Changing Lanes

A New Adult's Guide to Understanding your Lane in Life

BY
TONIA N. EAST

USA ▪ Canada ▪ UK ▪ Ireland

Unless otherwise indicated, Scripture quotations used in this book are from The Holy Bible, New King James Version (NKJV). Copyright © 1979,1980,1982,1990 Thomas Nelson, Inc., Publishers.
Also quoted:
The King James Version (KJV)
The New International Version (NIV), ©1973,1984 by International Bible Society.
Zondervan Bible Publishers.
The Amplified Bible (AMP), © 1954, 1958, 1962, 1964, 1965, 1987 by the Lockman Foundation.
Cover photo by G. Arnell Williams.

Note for Librarians: A cataloguing record for this book is available from Library and Archives Canada at www.collectionscanada.ca/amicus/index-e.html
ISBN 1-4120-6476-7

PUBLISHING

Offices in Canada, USA, Ireland and UK
This book was published *on-demand* in cooperation with Trafford Publishing. On-demand publishing is a unique process and service of making a book available for retail sale to the public taking advantage of on-demand manufacturing and Internet marketing. On-demand publishing includes promotions, retail sales, manufacturing, order fulfilment, accounting and collecting royalties on behalf of the author.

Book sales for North America and international:
Trafford Publishing, 6E–2333 Government St.,
Victoria, BC v8t 4p4 CANADA
phone 250 383 6864 (toll-free 1 888 232 4444)
fax 250 383 6804; email to orders@trafford.com
Book sales in Europe:
Trafford Publishing (uk) Limited, 9 Park End Street, 2nd Floor
Oxford, UK ox1 1hh UNITED KINGDOM
phone 44 (0)1865 722 113 (local rate 0845 230 9601)
facsimile 44 (0)1865 722 868; info.uk@trafford.com
Order online at:
trafford.com/05-1387

10 9 8 7 6 5 4 3 2

Contents

This book is dedicated to my father
Wallace M. East. Though you are no longer here,
your writing continues to live on in me.

Acknowledgements

First and foremost, I must thank my mother, who is my constant source of encouragement and support. Thank you for never limiting my dreams, but pushing me to dream even bigger. I love you so much and am so blessed to have you as my best friend. To my spiritual father, Bishop Long, thank you for continuously motivating me to be all that Christ has called me to be. I want to thank my brother, Brian, for always believing his little sister would do great things. Kanika, you are my sister for life; thank you for reading the first page to this book and running with it. I thank Mrs. Chagnovich, for forcing me to be a better writer. Benjamin, thank you so much for editing my manuscript and making my writing more polished and precise. My dear friend Angela, thank you for just being you and revealing Christ in your life. Joanna, thank you for inspiring me to continue writing. I want to thank Valorie Burton for kicking me in the butt and getting me in gear to publish my own book. Claudette, you are my prayer partner and my very own cheering squad; thanks for not giving up on me. Finally, I thank God for placing His Word in me, Holy Spirit for inspiration, and Jesus for laying His life down that I might live.

Introduction

Have you ever been driving somewhere and became completely lost? Not the kind of lost where you have some idea where you are going, but the kind of lost where you are not going to make it to your destination without help. Perhaps you look for help from someone who is familiar with where you need to go, but they too can lead you astray.

One evening I was driving home thinking about this or that and before I knew it, I had missed my exit. Now if you have lived in the country you realize that you can't just get right off, because the next exit might be miles away. It was getting late and I had only lived in Georgia for about a year at that time, so I didn't know many alternate routes. I did know that if I continued to go straight I would eventually come to another exit that I could take home. Unfortunately, this exit was about an hour away and in my impatience I decided to take a closer exit that I was somewhat familiar with. As I was driving down the interstate, I became hopelessly lost. It was getting close to midnight and I was in a deserted section of the interstate with no lights, no people, and no idea where I was going. I had not the slightest idea of how to get back on track. As my eyes began to well with tears of fear and confusion, I came to the conclusion that I must crush my pride and stop at a gas station to get directions. The attendant told me where to go but he didn't seem so sure of his answer. I followed his instructions and prayed that he was right. Though it took me almost an hour to find my way back, it was worth the lesson I learned on the journey.

Whether or not we have ever been physically lost, many of us face seasons where we feel spiritually lost. We have no idea where we are going or where we are supposed to be. This feeling can occur at various times in our lives: times of change, times of fear or sadness, or at times of disobedience, when we willfully choose to change from the lane God has placed us in. At these times it may feel as if we are all alone to figure out our way on our own. Only then do we realize that it really has nothing to do with our way or our will and everything to do with His way and His will. But what is God's will for your life? This is often the point where we feel most confused. In our impatience, instead of following the way we know we should go, we decide to take matters into our own hands and take a short cut or hop in the fast lane. As I found out, short cuts can take me so far off course that it ends up being much longer than if I would have taken the way that I knew was right. Many times the world makes it seem like God's way is so long and so hard, but without God's instruction life really gets hard. We are tempted to always be in the fast lane. The fast lane of the world can often lead us so far away from where God wants us to be that we go through unnecessary hardship that takes us longer than if we had kept the course God has for our lives.

As I thought about the many times I have been lost physically, two things had to happen before I could get back on track. First, I had to reach a point where I realized that I wasn't going to be able to find my way on my own; second, I had reached a point where I was either going to have to look at a map or talk to someone who knew where I needed to be. When we are spiritually lost, the same process must occur. If we are physically lost, the only reason we would refuse to look at a map or take advice from someone is because we are convinced that we do not need help, which is the result of our own pride in not wanting to admit we were wrong or because of our need to be in control.

When I was a teen I thought I knew everything. Every time my mother told me something, I would quickly retort, "I know, mom!" I thank God I had a patient mother, because I don't know if I would have been so tolerant of my foolish arrogance. When I look back, I realize I knew nothing and I realize how silly it was of me to reject my parent's wisdom. The same thing applies to our relationship with our heavenly Father. We often want to say to God, "I know, Father, but just let me do this." Praise God, He is patient with us as we think we know more than the Creator of the Universe. There is a saying: "If you want to make God laugh, tell Him your plans." God must have a good sense of humor to keep from getting frustrated and upset with us as we charge full force in the wrong direction and end up crashed and burned. We must realize that we need to receive God's instruction daily. We need to come to the point where we can surrender our will to God and realize that we are never going to reach our spiritual destination without His help.

Secondly, we need a map. When we look at a map not only can we see where we are, but where we've been, and where we need to go. God's word is our road map for life.

Psalm 119:105 states "Your word is a lamp to my feet and a light for my path." We can rest assured that wherever God wants us to go, He can lead us there by His word. In His word we can see where we made wrong turns in our past. God can also reveal what we need to do to keep from making the same mistakes. This is why we should continually read His word in order to take our next step in faith.

Some common excuses that we give to God are that we are too young or we do not have the ability to do what God has asked us to do. First, we must realize that God will not ask us to do anything that He has not equipped us to do. Secondly, we must realize that God's will is so much bigger than ours. We are just vessels that God can pour His spirit into, clay that He can mold. When God came to Jeremiah as a young man, He declared, "Before I formed you in the womb I knew you, before you were born I set you apart; I appointed you as a prophet to the nations"(Jer. 1:5). Jeremiah replies that he is only a child and he doesn't know how to speak. Now if God knows us and sets us apart before we are even born, we are not set apart for failure but for success. Not successful because of our own talent and ability, but because of God's faithfulness to His will in our lives. God replies to Jeremiah and tells him not to say that he is too young (he was actually about twenty) for Jeremiah **must** go to everyone that He sends him to and say whatever God tells him to say. In the New International Version, God tells Jeremiah that "you must go": He is telling Jeremiah that no one else can do the work that God has for him. God has also given us a purpose, a calling that he especially designed for us to do. We cannot pass it on to someone else or wait until tomorrow.

Many of us have been called at a young age to stand for God. So many young and new adults are hurting, hopeless, and in search of answers that are only in Christ Jesus.

God declares that He knows the plans He has for us and that they are plans to prosper us not to harm us, plans to give us a hope and a future. Thank God, we do not have to walk through life without hope or a future. If you do feel hopeless and depressed about your future, know that if you choose today to walk the journey God has for you, you will have hope and you will have a future. Yes, even after we've made the decision to walk with Christ we may feel discouraged, but this is because of our own lack of faith. The world encourages us to walk through life blindly into the snares of the enemy.

The goal of this book is to reveal how God has an assigned lane for our lives that will lead us away from the potholes of the world. This book is written especially for new adults who are tired of walking through life aimlessly. Although there are specific callings that God has for us individually, all paths should lead us to a closer walk with our Heavenly Father. Hopefully throughout this book we will learn how not to just stay in the smooth lane, but how to seek the best lane for our lives, while, learning how to overcome obstacles along the way. This book will make that possible by looking at various biblical figures and principles and how God reveals His perfect lane for our lives.

CHAPTER 1

Packing Light

JESUS INSTRUCTS US TO PACK LIGHT.

Do we really trust God enough to do whatever he has called us to do, without question? If God came to us today and said "I want you to go to this land and take no money, no credit cards, no traveler's checks, no luggage, but I will appoint people on the way to be a blessing to you", I know my first reaction would be "Lord is that you?" This type of call forces us not to trust in our own ability to be prepared, but to completely trust in God. After giving the disciples power and authority to drive out demons and cure diseases, Jesus sent out his disciples to minister to the "lost sheep of Israel" (Matt 10:1-6). He gave them specific directions as to what they were to take on their journey. He tells them, "Do not take along any gold or silver or copper in your belts; take no bag for the journey, or extra tunic, or sandals or a staff; for the worker is worth his keep" (Matt 10: 7-10).

This verse became much more real to me when I went backpacking in Europe. Though I tried to pack as light as possible, I found myself becoming fatigued when we had to walk for long distances. Not only did my friend and I grow tired of the weight, it literally caused us pain. We began to avoid going places if we knew that we would have to carry our packs for a while. Though the disciples may have not realized it at the time, Jesus was only looking after their best interests. They would be free to travel long distances without additional weight slowing them down, most importantly, they would learn to depend on God to meet all their needs. We cry out to God, but we still depend on our own resources. God would love to intervene, but we will not let Him remove our dependence on people, things, and ourselves. It is only when we come to God in helplessness that He can move miraculously in our lives.

After living in California all of my life, God began to reveal to me that I would not live in California for much longer. I had no idea where I was going, but wherever it was I had a feeling that the land would be lush with trees. When I was preparing to go to graduate school, I applied all over the country not knowing where I was going to go or whether I should even go to graduate school. I was already heavily in debt from my undergraduate degree and I told the Lord "If it is your will for me to go to graduate school you will be Jehovah Jireh and provide everything I need. As with college, I will know where you want me to go by the doors you will open." The very first response stated that I did receive a full scholarship. After my first week in Georgia I knew this was where I was supposed to be. Yes, I did have challenges, but I knew that God did not bring me this far to leave me now. God will give us favor when we follow His will, but the enemy will also try and deceive us to believe that something we know is the will of God was actually our own decision. Proverbs 3:5-6 instructs us to

> *Trust in the Lord with all your heart, and lean not on your own understanding; in all your ways acknowledge Him and He shall direct your paths.*

When we trust in God with all our heart we are called to do things beyond ourselves. Things that we would have never thought of or even considered to be possible, are possible in Christ Jesus. But as we continue to follow Him we see how He has made our paths straight. God is not the author of confusion. Many times when we find ourselves twisting and turning, we are not on God's path at all. The road to God is straight and narrow. Then why is it difficult? Because we must completely rely on God and there's no room for us to bring along our own baggage of sin, pride, lust, or independence. Jesus tells us that "small is the gate and narrow is the road that leads to life" (Matt. 7:13). When we feel that we must be accepted by others and are more concerned with the cares of this world, we cannot see God's path for the path that we have allowed the world to put us on. When God tells us to pack light, we must be confident in His provision. He will make our paths straight when we trust in Him with all of our heart.

In order to trust in the Lord with **all** our heart, our heart must be full of God above anything else. This means we must remove the baggage of life: the hurts, the worries, the stress, the sin, and anything else that might take up room in our heart that should be reserved for God. I know I have often let my own desires consume my heart without even realizing what I was doing. One of my dear friends once gave a message that forced me to analyze the excess baggage that I was carrying in my life. If we have hurts from past relationships, unforgiveness, bitterness, anger, or doubts, these must be removed before we can truly allow God to reign in our heart. How can we come to God and ask Him to forgive us, when we have not forgiven others? If Christ can forgive those that crucified Him there shouldn't be anything that we are not able to forgive. When Jesus was teaching the disciples how they ought to pray, he tells them to ask, "Forgive us our debts, as we also have forgiven our debtors."(Matt. 6:12) When He says, "have forgiven" it is in the past tense, suggesting that forgiveness has already been given before we come to our Father in prayer. It is the prayers of the righteous that avails much (James 5:16). We cannot come to God with wrath and dissension in our heart. Jesus tells us to love our enemies and to pray for those that mistreat us (Matt 5:43-44). When we lean not to our own understanding, we may not always understand why, but we know that in the end God will be glorified.

In order to trust in God and not our own understanding, we must step out of our comfort zones. Oftentimes, we refuse to step out of our comfort zones voluntarily, but God allows us to go through times of discomfort in order for us to seek the will of God on this journey. During my childhood I was very blessed and I praise God for His blessing, but I also praise Him for the trials. I was definitely a Daddy's girl and my father was the epitome of strength and security. At the age of thirteen I watched my father's life wither before my eyes. Not until I lost my father was I able to put my faith completely in my Heavenly Father's hand. His death also taught me not to take for granted the lives of those who are still a blessing to me today.

Another time in my life when I grew closer in my walk with God was when I moved out on my own. Though I lived away from home in college, I was still only a drive away from the security of home. I knew that if there was anything I needed I could just go home. However, when I moved to Georgia I was over 2,000 miles away from home, family, and friends. I didn't know anyone in Georgia and my nearest friend was in Tennessee. However, I think that it is in the times when we are alone with God that He reveals Himself to us. Have you ever had a really bad day and wanted to talk with someone but no one was home? It is when we turn to God that we realize that He is a friend that is always there, no matter what time it is, no matter where we are in the world. At one point I didn't know how I was going to make it. I hadn't found a church home and felt really disconnected. I needed God to bless me financially; bills were pouring in and I didn't know how they were going to be paid. Not until I was on my own did God allow me to go through a process of preparation: in my lack of resources did I see the salvation of the Lord. I believe that there are times in our lives when God allows us to be stripped of some comforts, in order for us to walk with Him more closely as our faith is strengthened and we seek Him wholeheartedly.

In times of trial we also have a testimony that God can use to encourage someone else or to enable us to relate with someone else's struggle. We are able to share how the Holy

Spirit comforted us and how weeping may endure for a night, but joy comes in the morning (Ps. 30:5). Because Satan had tempted Jesus in His earthly body, Jesus has compassion and understanding when we cry out to Him. Jesus can do more than sympathize and provide support and understanding: He can also empathize with our trials and struggles. However, we could never empathize with the pain he bore for us. Sometimes on this journey, you need someone that can empathize with you and let you know how they made it through. However, if we don't ever make it through anything we will never be able to encourage someone else in that way. For example, I can empathize with those who have lost a parent at a young age and let them know that with God's help He will ease the pain. Yes, there are always moments of sadness, but God's love gives a continual joy that endures day after day.

Sometimes God must also strip us in order for us to be removed from a path of sin. I can remember times in my childhood when my parents would not allow me to be around certain environments or people that they knew were not beneficial in my life. Our Heavenly Father must allow us to be removed from certain environments and people that are not beneficial to the path God has planned for us. He will not force us to leave these environments, but he will reveal to us why they are not beneficial in our lives. When we continue to stay in environments of sin, discouragement, and pain we take on more baggage than we were ever intended to carry. We ask God why must life be so hard, but when He has given us a way out, we refuse to take it. Once God has removed this baggage of sin we should not accumulate more along the way.

CARRY YOUR OWN LOAD

Many times our load becomes too much to bear when we feel that it is our duty to carry the load for everyone. Only Jesus had the power and the strength to take on the sins of the entire nation. When we come before God on Judgment Day He will put our own works to the fire to see if they were pure and we will not be responsible for the works of others, not even our children. God promises us that He would never put more on us than we could bear, and what He does put on us is only to make us stronger in Him. Not only must we put our lives in His hands, but also the lives of those we care about. In I Peter 5:17, we are told to cast **all** our cares upon Him, because he cares for us. It's good to know that God is willing to take on **all** my cares, not just a few. This not only includes the cares we have for our own growth with God, but the cares we have for others.

In my own life I have always been sensitive to others' feelings, needs, desires, which is both a help and hindrance to ministry. Yes, I believe that we must have true compassion for others as Jesus had for us, but it must be released. As we notice the pain in the eyes of others or the sadness in their spirit I feel we should not ignore it; we should do something. The first thing we must do is pray and sometimes that's all we can do. If we should do more God will reveal that as well, but He will be glorified in what we do. Many times in relationships people begin to serve the needs of others and not the needs of God. Even in ministry, it is possible to focus on serving the church, not the Lord. No one should come before our relationship with our Heavenly Father. Our emotional back is breaking as we strain to carry everyone's cares and refuse to let Jesus lend us a hand. Jesus tells us to

> *Come to me, all you who are weary and burdened and I will give you rest. Take my yoke upon you and learn from me, for I am gentle and humble in heart, and you will find rest from your souls. For my yoke is easy and my burden is light.*

> (Matt. 11:28-30, NIV)

THE ONE THING YOU CAN'T LEAVE HOME WITHOUT.

Oftentimes, as we prepare for a trip or vacation we end up packing more than we need, or could ever use in the short period we are there. On our spiritual journey we are likely to have the same excessive baggage, taking on more cares, worries, and material possessions than we need or could ever use in our lifetime. So what are the essentials we must have on this spiritual journey? The one thing we need to have is a spiritual map to lead us on this journey. When I am going somewhere that I have never been before the first thing I grab before going out the door is the directions. There is nothing worse than rushing out the door and realizing you are driving aimlessly because, in your haste, you have forgotten to bring the directions and must return home to retrieve them. In our busy lives we often forget to ask God for His directions. Our Father knows that we need His directions, which is why we must have His word on this journey. If you were in a business where you would have to drive somewhere new every day, it would be important that you always had a good map along and consulted it daily. As you continue to use the map the directions will become ingrained in your mind. Each day we live we will come across new obstacles, new people, and new ideas. Without consulting God's word daily, we are bound to become lost and not even realize it until we are so far off the path God has for us, we long for His presence and guidance once again. This is why it is necessary that we daily ask God to show us His will through prayer and by the guidance of His word. As we continually consult God's word His directions will begin to be embedded in our spirit and we will follow it unconsciously. His word becomes like a familiar drive home. I revealed earlier how I initially was lost on my way home, but now I can drive home and unconsciously make the right turns because it has become a habitual pattern.

Our dependence upon God's word should be so much a part of our lives that it becomes our spiritual food that our souls cannot live without. I don't know about you, but I don't miss too many meals. The only time I will consciously not eat is if God says that something can only be done through prayer and fasting. Normally, my body is used to receiving three meals a day, so generally around the same times I find myself becoming hungry. Our souls should hunger for God's word as our body hungers for food. "As the deer pants for streams of water so my soul pants for you, O God" (Ps. 42:1). The more we meditate on God's word the more we will prosper. Psalms 1reads,

*Blessed is the man who walks not in the counsel of the
ungodly, nor stands in the path of sinners, nor sits in
the seat of the scornful; But his delight is in the law of
the Lord, and on His law he meditates day and night.
(Ps. 1:1-2)*

This Psalm reveals how our journey will be blessed as we seek
God's word and not the counsel of the wicked. Oftentimes,
when we must make important decisions we go to our closest or most respected friends. However, if God does not lead
these friends they can lead us astray. The best thing to do
is to seek God first in His word and in prayer, and He will
reveal to us where it is we need to go. More and more God is
revealing to me that I should not be so quick to give advice,
unless I have prayed about it or clearly see God's will. If we
really don't know, we should not say "this is what I would
do", but just say, "Pray about it." Therefore we are not creating dependence upon us, but upon God. Though, God can
speak to us through other people, as He does in the Bible, we
should not be quick to ask others for advice, especially when
they are not led by God.

LET NOTHING HINDER YOU

In Hebrews 12:1 we are instructed to "lay aside every
weight, and the sin which so easily ensnares us." Hebrews
provides guidance as to how we should not be burdened
down by past or present sin in our life. This scripture instructs us to remove every weight, which is an excellent il-
lustration. One day I was asked by one of my students to
bring weights to school for a project she was doing. I had

forgotten they were in my bag and wondered why I was so tired as I walked up the stairs until I remembered I had these weights in my bag. We often wonder why we are spiritually tired in this Christian journey, when we refuse to remove the weight of sin in our life. We continue to drag it with us everywhere we go, not able to go higher in God's will because spiritual weights are holding us down.

Christ has promised us, "who the son sets free is free indeed"(John 8:36). It is not God's will for us to be bound by anything. In fact, it is impossible for us to do the will of God when we are bound by sin, which is why Christ died on the cross to set us free. Yet, we bind ourselves in worry, sin, and fear. However, if we believe that God will do what He has promised to do in our lives then there is no need to worry, no need to fear, no need to give in to sin. Our faith is what will set us free, for it is impossible to please God without faith (Heb. 11: 6). Why is faith the one thing we need to please God: what about our works? Our works are in vain if we do them with faith in ourselves and not in God. We may say we're doing it in God's name when we really are depending on our own wisdom, or talent, or resources. Faith is substance of things hoped for, the evidence of things we cannot see (Heb. 11:1). If we know how it is going to work out then it doesn't require faith. So when we don't know how it is going to turn out and we cannot rely on our own wisdom (because we are confused), our own talent (because it is insufficient), or our own resources (because they are not enough), and we turn to God and say "I know that you will make a way because you are El Shaddai, the one who is more than enough" – that requires faith. This is what pleases God:

when we let go of our independence and completely depend on Him. When we realize that we are weak and were not built to carry all these burdens, then we must call on Jehovah Jireh, our provider. Our load will always be too much to bear when we try to carry everything ourselves. If you want to be free, let go and let God. We must know that God has a purpose for our lives and He will bring it to pass, we just have to believe and be obedient.

1. Are there cares that are weighing you down spiritually?

2. How can you begin to give those cares to God?

Prayer

Father, *I praise you for being Jehovah Jireh my provider, the reason why I don't have to worry because you will give me everything I need. Jehovah Shalom, my peace, the reason why I don't have to fear; as long as I am in your will I can rest in you. Jehovah Rohi, my shepherd, that when I am confused you will lead and show me your way. All I need is in your name, Jesus. I thank you for setting me free from the bondage of sin, fear, and worry. When you sent your Son to die for me He took on all our cares, all sickness, all sin that we might live life and live it more abundantly. I pray that I do not allow myself to become overwhelmed by my own independence, sin, or desire to please others. Christ died so that I might be free and I will walk in the freedom you died for me to obtain. I pray that I will love others, as my self. I pray your forgiveness of all my sins as I have forgiven others. I thank you for your mercy. I thank you for your grace. I thank you for freedom in Christ Jesus. Amen.*

CHAPTER 2

Follow the Leader

In order to be available for God to use us, we must be willing to follow God's lead. We are not going to be able to follow God's lead until we are willing to sacrifice. God needs to know that there is nothing in life more important than Him. Nothing. Oftentimes, we want to receive God's very best blessings, yet we refuse to give Him our best sacrifice. God will withhold no good thing from those that love him and obey him. However, we cannot say that we love Him if we are not obeying what He has called us to do. Jesus tells us plainly that if we love Him we will obey His commandments and if we don't we do not love Him (John 14:23-24).

ABRAHAM FOLLOWS GOD'S LEAD

God made a covenant with Abram that He would enlarge his family and allow them to be very fruitful, that he would be the "father of many nations" and he would no longer be called Abram, but Abraham (Gen. 17:5). Not only does God make His covenant with Abram individually, but to generations to come. This covenant would not include the son who had come, Ishmael. Though Ishmael would be blessed, this promise is not for him. He promises Abraham that Sarah will be the mother of kings. Abraham laughs, in doubt, at the thought that Sarah would conceive a child at the age of ninety. Then God states, "Sarah your wife shall bear a son indeed and you shall call his name Isaac " (Gen. 17:19). Can you imagine the joy that Abraham must have felt after the revelation of such tremendous blessing? Though, the world would call for celebration, God called for sacrifice. When God promises that He is going to do something in our lives, it does not mean we can sit back and watch the blessings roll in. We must immediately prepare to receive that blessing. On the same day that Abraham heard this word from God he and all the males of his house were circumcised, including those that he had bought from foreign lands. It is revealed that every male was circumcised "as God had said to him" (Gen. 17:23). Many times when God tells us to do something, we hesitate and try to rationalize or compromise the word of God. Abraham acted immediately, but he did not compromise by allowing his workers to not be circumcised. Abraham was blessed as he boldly declared by his actions, "As for me and my house, we will serve the Lord!" Abraham was ninety-nine years old when he was circumcised, so it's obvious that he was not comfortable. Even in Abraham's old age he was not so set in his ways that he would not obey God. Can you imagine what his foreign workers must have been thinking? Whatever they were thinking they had to get over it or hit the road, because every male was circumcised. Oftentimes, I know for myself, I try to make others feel comfortable even if I'm not. However, God will call us to do things that will not only upset our apple cart, but those

around us as well, so He can be glorified. In order to prepare
to receive the blessing of God Abraham sanctified himself as
well as his environment.

If we do not adequately prepare ourselves for the tremendous blessings of God we will begin to worship the blessing
and not the 'blessor.' At last, the desire of Abraham's heart
was finally fulfilled. I'm sure that it was a joyous day on the
day Isaac was born. Abraham was blessed because of his
faith and obedience to God. There are promises that God has
made to each of us and, like Abraham, it may appear to be
hopeless to some, but nothing is impossible for God. As we
are faithful and obey God, we will be blessed.

God has to know that He can trust us with the blessing.
Even after God had blessed Abraham with Isaac, Abraham
had to prove that he would not exalt Isaac above the will
of God. God tells Abraham to "Take your son, Isaac, whom
you love, and go to the regions of Moriah. Sacrifice him
there as a burnt offering on one of the mountains I will tell
you about"(Gen. 22:2). I found it to be interesting that God
would note Abraham's love for Isaac. Naturally a father
would love his son, but perhaps God questioned whether
his love for Isaac was greater than his love for Him. When
we note someone's love for someone it is often done in the
form of a question, such as if someone says, "If you really
loved me, then you would …". Once again Abraham reveals
his love, as he does not hesitate upon God's word. **Early** the
next morning Abraham arose to start on his journey to Mt.
Moriah. Abraham did not ponder on God's word and try to
think of reasonable excuses. Abraham did not say, "I am too
old to travel for such a long distance." The land of Moriah

was about fifty miles away and would take him at least three days to get there. When God has called us to go on a difficult journey, we often think that it must be the enemy. But it is God who tests us in ways that will bring us closer to Him, while the enemy wants us to be led away from God's will. Abraham could have disobeyed God by saying that God would not ask him to give up his beloved son, the son that would fulfill the covenant. This was truly a difficult test for Abraham, but was made easier as he passed subsequent tests. When Abram was 75 years old he obediently followed God as he told him to leave his country, where all his family was, and go to a land that He would show to him. Can you imagine packing up and not even knowing where you are going? As he passed subsequent test his faith was strengthened, enabling him to pass greater tests.

When Abraham arrived in Moriah he tells his servants, "Stay here with the donkey while I and the boy go over there. We will worship and then we will come back to you" (Gen. 22:8). Abraham planned to give his son as a sacrificial praise offering to God, the best that he had to give. John (4:24) reveals to us how we must worship the Father in spirit and in truth. Abraham's flesh may not have wanted to offer his son up, but his spirit followed the will of God and his faith allowed him to worship him in truth. Sometimes we take worship too lightly and think that it will always be easy and make us feel good. Abraham revealed what it truly means to worship the Father in spirit and in truth. Abraham did not grudgingly follow the word of God. He followed God, having faith that even if Isaac must be resurrected God's word would be fulfilled. Notice how Abraham declares to his servants "we will come back" not "I will come back." Abraham knew that God would fulfill His covenant and can move in what looks like an impossible situation. Even if God must raise Isaac from the dead, Abraham knew that His covenant with God would not be broken. God will fulfill every word He has spoken to us, if we only believe.

Abraham prepares the wood for the burnt offering, binds Isaac, and places him on the altar. As he takes the knife to slay his son, the angel of the Lord tells him not to harm his son. Abraham looks up and sees a ram caught in the thicket. As Abraham sacrifices the ram, he names that place Jehovah Jireh, the Lord will provide. Why do you think the angel of the Lord waited until the very moment before Isaac would be sacrificed? Perhaps it revealed how serious Abraham was about following the will of God. After the angel stops him at the point of death, he states that "Now I know that you fear God, because you have not withheld from me your son, your only son" (Gen. 22:12). He goes on to declare, "that because you have you have done this … I will surely bless you and make your descendents as numerous as the stars in the sky and the sand on the seashore." If God had any question of Abraham's love before, at that moment He was convinced that He could bless him tremendously and it would not affect his love for Him. The question now is would God be so convinced of our love for Him?

Though we may not be called to literally sacrifice someone, we are often required to release someone to God. My mother once told me that there was a time when my brother and I could literally make her physically sick from worrying over the many things we did or could have happened. Then one day she realized she had to release us to God, because she could not carry our load any longer. Though I know she loves us unconditionally, she will not allow us to steal her joy or peace. Perhaps it isn't your children, but your friends, your boss, your boyfriend or girlfriend, your husband or wife. We often allow others to come before God, including ourselves. Instead of following God's directions we serve ourselves and not God. If Abraham would have served himself he would not have arose early the next morning: he would have allowed the flesh to talk him into staying in bed just a little longer. Then if he continued to serve himself, he would have said that, "I cannot travel such a distance. I am over a hundred years old and I can't do what I used to do." There are things that God has called us to do and we often make every excuse in the world for not doing it. It may be something small, such as getting up early to pray and study God's word, so that you can know what His directions are for that day. But we linger in bed and before we know it's time to go to work, to school, to get something to eat. If God can't trust us to do small things, how could He trust us with an enormous blessing? He states in his word that,

> He that is faithful in that which is least is faithful also
> in much: and he that is unjust in the least is unjust also
> in much. (Luke 16:10)

We wonder why we have not received God's abundant blessing and it's because He is not convinced that it will not come before our relationship with Him. As we are faithful to God in the small things, He will give us bigger responsibilities. We cannot say "Lord I want to be a witness for you all over the world", when we do not witness to our class-mates, our friends, or our co-workers we see every day. My former pastor once gave a message revealing how we cannot be successful leaders until we become successful followers. Many want to lead before they learn to follow. You may feel frustrated in what you're doing for God right now and think that you should do more, but He is preparing you for big-ger things as you are faithful in smaller things. Sometimes I thought I was ready to take on more and God had to whisper in my ear "Be still and know that I am God." We must learn to wait patiently on God. However, we are not waiting idly: we are learning to become excellent waiters or waitresses. As we wait on God we make sure that He has everything He needs and serve Him with gratitude. One day God will give us a big order, but we must be faithful in serving the drinks and appetizers before He can trust us with the main dish.

As we wait on God we must never doubt His will for our lives and what God has promised us. God's promise to Abraham's son Israel is the same promise God has made to us. Paul reminds us that we are not children of Hagar, as Ishmael was: we were not born into slavery. We are the children of Sarah, as Israel was, and we share in His inheri-tance. Everything we will ever have need of is already ours in Christ Jesus; we just have to ask God in faith and He will provide it in the right time. Paul declares that we "are chil-dren of promise" (Gal. 4: 28). God has given us a promise of blessing, of freedom, of hope. This is why we should not let ourselves be weighed down by sin when we think of all the things God wants to do in our lives. God is faithful: to complete what He has begun in us, we just have to trust in

Him and stand on His promise. We also must follow God's instructions in the little things so that we will be prepared to receive His promise for our lives.

1. Is there anything that you would not willingly sacrifice to God?

2. What can you begin doing to trust God more completely?

Prayer

Father, I praise you for being and all-knowing God. There is nothing that will occur in my life that has not already occurred to you. Before I was born you knew your purpose for me and you called me to do your will. I pray that I will never doubt your will for my life, no matter what I must overcome. For I know that your plan for my life is for good and not for evil, to give me hope and a future. I praise you Father for being omnipresent, that no matter where I am you are there. You will never leave me, nor forsake me. No matter who turns against me, I can always turn to you and you will comfort me and give me strength to do your will. I pray that I will not take credit for the blessings in my life, for all that is good and perfect comes from you. I also pray that I will not be jealous or hinder the blessing in another's life. I pray that you lead me, for you promised that you would be my shepherd. I cannot take one step without your guidance and direction in my life. As you show me the way that I should go let me walk in boldness, without fear. Not because of who I am, but because of who you are in me. Amen.

CHAPTER 3

The Wide Road

It's a tie score, 88-88, with 3 minutes left in the fourth quarter. Fans are shouting for their teams. Your team, The Conquerors, is favored to win the championship. Though Jesse, your point guard, is one of the best, he will need a full team effort to win. Jesse passes the basketball to Tim and Tim passes the ball to Sam. Sam is in perfect position to shoot. He lifts the ball as if he is about to take the shot, but in fear he passes it back to Jesse. Though Jesse is surrounded defensively, he is able to pump fake and make the shot anyway. The other team calls a timeout. Your coach again shows the team what they need to do in order to win. Jesse, who is also the captain, reminds your team how close you are to winning the championship but it is going to take a full team effort. The buzzer sounds. The players take their position on the court. On the bench sit some players that are encouraging their team from the sidelines, some players sitting on the bench ready for their opportunity to go in, some players that are just happy to be on a winning team, and some players who are not disappointed or excited: they're just there. Back on the court, star players like Jesse were doing all they could to win but without the help of most of the team they were unable to seize a victory.

I know you might be asking yourself "what does this have to do with staying in the lane God has placed me in?" Well the day you decided to be a Christian, you became part of a winning team. Your Bible contains every play you will need to know. It also gives us the tactics of the opposing team. Every day we have the opportunity to practice the instructions we've been given. However, our coach will not force us to. We must practice what we believe, not because we know we should do so, but because of our love for who we serve. Good players are those that are passionate both in and out of the game. They are just as dedicated to being the best in practice and in their own individual workouts as they are in the game. The game just shows the fruit of their labor. As Christians we have to be passionate for our walk with Christ, not just when we are in church or Bible study but everyday. We may wear the Christian Jersey and talk the lingo, but is our heart really in the game?

One thing we must continually strive to overcome is complacency. Like Jesse, there will always be star players in church that do everything while the rest of the congregation sits back and watch. Or maybe others in your family play more active roles in the church, but their faith will not get you into heaven. Though we are not all called to be out front, we are called to do something. God has given us all talents and abilities that strengthen the body of Christ. Even when on the bench you can play an important role in encouraging your team. Though we may be on the bench, we need to be ready for when God calls on us. Perhaps we are just satisfied with being on a winning team, but that's not good enough. We should not be so content in our own salvation that we are not trying to recruit others to be Conquerors for Christ. Or are we like the players on the bench that are neither disappointed nor excited about being on the team: are we just here for the ride? A word from God was given to the church of Laodicea about their complacency, saying

> I know your deeds, that you are neither cold nor hot. I wish you were either one or the other! So because you are lukewarm –neither hot nor cold – I am about to spit you out of my mouth. (Rev. 3:15-16, NIV)

These may appear to be rather stern words when their church was not really doing anything wrong, but they weren't doing anything right either. When we become complacent we are actually giving place to Satan. How? By not diligently seeking God's purpose in our life we have become unfaithful stewards. The enemy has come to steal, kill, and destroy. We can allow him to steal our faith, kill God's plan for our life, and destroy every spiritual blessing God would love to give us with our complacency. In the earlier analogy, Sam had the perfect shot and the ability to make it, but he didn't because he was scared. Like Sam, God has given us the perfect shot but we must have faith to take it. God is constantly revealing things that we need to do for Him. We must choose which team we are going to be on. Just because we go to church does not mean that we are on God's team. Jesus warned the disciples that though the Pharisees may appear to be on God's team, "Everything they do is done for men to see" (Matt. 23:5). Are we serving man or are we serving God? Many times when we choose to serve God man will turn against us. You see, the Lukewarm Road allows you to be popular with the church and with the world, but not with God. You can receive the benefits of being on the team but you aren't taking an active role, which is a benefit to the opposing team. Jesus stated, "He who is not with me is against me" (Matt 12:30). So either we are standing for God or we are standing for the prince of this world. There is no in between. Faith is not a toy that we can play with for a while and then put away until the next Sunday. Our Father seeks those that will worship Him in spirit and in truth and we can only do that when we seek His will on a daily basis, not just on Sunday.

> *Neither do men light a lamp and put it under a basket,*
> *but on a lampstand; and it gives light to all that are in*
> *the house. Let your light so shine before men, that they*
> *may see your good works, and glorify your Father in*
> *heaven.(Matt. 5:15-16)*

When we are complacent we are not letting our light shine. If it is shining it's just a flicker. Just enough light to say, "Hey, I'm a Christian!" But not enough light to lead people out of darkness. When we are in church we may let our little light shine, but it's more vital that it shine when we are at school, at work, with our friends, at the mall, wherever there is darkness. Have you ever been in a situation when you knew that what was being said or done was not right, but you didn't say anything in fear of offending the other person? I know I have. God revealed to me that when I do this, essentially I am hiding my light under a bushel. Oh no!

I remember as a child singing "I'm gonna' let it shine, let it shine, let it shine!" Somehow when we get older we forget to apply this song to our lives in order to be liked by everyone. However, we must fear God and not man. I learned that oftentimes their reaction is not as bad as I thought it would be. If it is said in love, whether or not they agree, they still know you care. I am so grateful for my friends who held me accountable when I was not letting my light shine. Once when I was going to the beach with my friend, we were in the parking lot and someone cut me off or something that made me upset. My initial reaction did not let my light shine and she said something to me like "That was real Christ-like." I was defensive at first, but to this day I try not to be as impatient on the road, especially when people cut me off.

How do we know if we are traveling down the lukewarm road? Though we will always be tempted to sin, it's our desire that will let us know if we are heading down the wrong road. We were all born into sin, but when we accepted Christ as our Savior and received the power of the Holy Spirit, we were no longer slaves to sin. Paul explains how our flesh and our spirit are at war. We desire to do what is good, yet are flesh wants to partake in sin. Paul explains,

> For in my inner being I delight in God's law; but I see another law at work in the members of my body waging war against the law of my mind ... Who will rescue me from this body of death? Thanks be to God- through Jesus Christ our Lord. (Rom. 7:22-25, NIV)

Well if Jesus has rescued us from the power of sin, why is it that we still stumble in sin? It is because we have allowed the desire of our flesh to become more important than our desire to serve God. Notice how Paul states that the war is in our minds. It's crucial that we realize how important it is to hold every thought captive and analyze whether or not it supports the will of God in our life. It is often said that the road to hell is paved by good intentions. We can have every intention to do good, but we must act accordingly. We may intend to do what is right, but if we keep allowing our minds to be filled with thoughts contrary to the will of God, our flesh will overtake us. When Eve was tempted in the garden, she allowed her desire to be like God to overtake her desire to obey God. Adam allowed his desire to please his only companion pull him away from God. Yet, when Jesus was tempted he never faltered. Why? Because his desire to please God was greater than any temptation that Satan could offer. When we desire to fulfill the lust of our flesh more than we desire to do the will of our Father, we just entered lukewarm road.

Jesus was not deceived by the enemy and could see the ugliness behind the beauty of what Satan offered. We must continually seek God's guidance and discernment in our lives, where we begin to see sin as He sees it, when we realize that, regardless of any momentary pleasure it may produce, it will eventually lead to our death. Adam and Eve saw the beauty of the apple, but not the poison it contained. When Esau, gave his birthright to Jacob for a bowl of soup all he could see was the temporary fulfillment and not the long-term consequences. However, when Joseph was tempted by Pharoah's wife he may have desired her, but he desired God's will more. If you have ever fasted for any period of time, though your body may desire food, you do not eat because your desire for God's will is stronger. We will always be tempted but we will not succumb to the temptation when the Holy Spirit gives us eyes to see that God's will is so much better.

IS HE REALLY LORD?

In church we sing songs about how much we love the Lord, but is He really our Lord? Does He have absolute authority in our life? If you're like me your automatic reaction is to say, "Yes, of course He does." However, when we begin to analyze our decisions on a daily basis our answer may differ. If He is our Lord, then we should seek His will on our jobs, in our relationships, and in every decision we make. It so tempting to just go with what we know or what we feel is right. However, the Word tells us not to lean on our understanding but to acknowledge God in all our ways and He will make our paths straight (Prov. 3:5). Though I have read this verse time and time again, I am still tempted to lean to my own understanding. The world is constantly telling us that if it looks good, tastes good, feels good, or all the above, it must be good. But like the saying says, everything that shines ain't gold. Have you found yourself looking back at mistakes that could have been avoided if you had sought God's will and not your own? On this journey we will have to take many important decisions, such as decisions about college, careers, marriage, and family. Without God's guidance we will inevitably make many mistakes, but if we let God order our steps whatever we do will prosper. It is when we acknowledge Him by letting our light shine that He

clears the path for His will in our lives. We can do nothing
apart from God.

> *I am the vine; you are the branches. If a man remains in
> me and I in him, he will bear much fruit; apart from me
> you can do nothing. (John 15: 13)*

MAKING HIM LORD

Surrender. Constantly realizing that we can do nothing
apart from Christ is essential. I believe that it is when we feel
independence from God that our faith begins to waver. It is
when we don't know where to go or what to do next that
we can humbly turn to God. Without faith it is impossible to
please our Lord. The less faith we place in our own abilities,
the more available we are to be used by God. If He is going
to be Lord in our life we must surrender all in order that His
will be done. We cannot pray effectively if we are still trying to manipulate the situation for our good. Basically, we
are not praying for His will to be done: we are praying for
our will to be done and proceed to tell Him exactly how it
should be done. Prayer is meaningless without dependence.
If we could do it on our own, why come to God? However,
we must realize we can do nothing that is lasting apart from
the will of God.

Sometimes, like Jonah, we know what we have been
called to do and try to run from God. Jonah never stopped
believing in God, but when God told him to go to Ninevah
and preach against the wickedness there, he hopped on a
ship and headed for Tarshish. Perhaps Jonah even had a
desire to preach in Tarshish, which would be a good thing

to do, but not what God called him to do. We often think that as long as we are doing a good thing we are in God's will, but we are still in disobedience. Why didn't Jonah want to preach to the people of Ninevah? He knew that God is gracious and compassionate and Jonah didn't believe that the people of Ninevah should receive God's mercy. Some of you may be saying, "how could Jonah not want others to receive God's grace," but do we not do the same thing? We go to church and give God praise. Yet, when God tells us to forgive someone we say, "No, Lord they don't deserve your love and mercy." First of all it should be impossible to say "No" to someone we say is "Lord" over our life. If He is Lord, it would mean that He reigns. Yet, even if we say no or just don't do it He still reigns and we have to suffer the consequences of being disobedient as Jonah did.

While Jonah was on the ship God sent a mighty wind that caused a great storm about the ship. All of the sailors knew that someone must be at fault for this to occur and began to cast lots to see which one was in the wrong. Of course the lot fell on Jonah and in their terror they asked, "What have you done?" (Jonah1:10). Jonah told them to pick him up and throw him into the sea and then the storm will become calm. God sent a great fish to swallow him up. Perhaps Jonah was prepared to meet a watery grave as he praised God in the fish's belly, stating

> In my distress I called to the Lord and he answered me.
> From the depths of the grave I called for help and you
> listened to my cry. (Jonah 2:2)

At least Jonah was obedient to the second call from God. If he hadn't been, not only would his life been in danger, but the lives of all of the sailors on the ship. Because of his obedience the sailors were convinced that Jonah's God must be the one true God and they gave him praise. Sometimes we, on the other hand, are so stubborn that we allow ourselves to be completely taken under before we turn to the Lord. Not only have we suffered in our disobedience, but also many others such as friends and family. I used to think that it was difficult to live for God until I began to see that it's so much harder not to. We must not attempt to take short cuts or change lanes, because it inevitably makes the journey much longer and tedious than if we had followed God's instructions from the start.

When we surrender to God we no longer surrender to sin. Yes we will be tempted, but sin has no power over us unless we allow it to, once we have surrendered to Christ. So do not feel you are weak because of your dependence on God; it is then that you are made strong. Paul reveals that sometimes God must allow us to endure pain to keep us from becoming conceited. He compares his hardship to a thorn in his flesh. Though he pleaded with God to remove his pain, God's reply was, "My grace is sufficient for your, for my power is made perfect in your weakness" (II Cor. 12:9). Therefore, Paul concluded that he would boast not in his strengths, but in his weaknesses. "For when I am weak, then am I strong"(II Cor. 12:10).

Get to know Him. We need to know the character of our Lord to serve Him effectively. Throughout the Bible God reveals the various dimensions in which He serves as Lord in our lives. God says whatever we ask in His name will be given to us, so we must understand what we possess in Him. To Abraham, He was revealed as Jehovah Jireh, the one who provides (Gen. 22:8). However, God also reveals Himself as a provider in the New Testament as well. Jesus explains in Matthew why we should not worry about how we will attain material possessions, when our Father knows exactly what we need and when we need it. Our main focus should be on seeking His kingdom and what we need will be given to us. So we can come to our Lord expecting that He will provide for every need. We just need to recognize whether it is something we need or something we want. Though God does bless us above what we need, if He knows if it will affect our love for Him He may withhold the want.

To Moses, God proved Himself to be the Jehovah Nissi, the Lord our Banner (Ex. 17:5). This is God's promise to protect us from our enemies. We have a right to go to our Lord for protection. When Saul sought to kill David, the Lord put up a banner of protection around him. When we seek to do God's will and obey His commands He will protect us. Not only will He protect us: He will give us victory. When King Jehoshaphat was afraid to go to battle the Lord sent a word to him saying,

> Do not be afraid nor dismayed because of this great multitude, for the battle is not yours, but God's. (II Ch. 20:15)

To David, the Lord was shown to be Jehovah Rohi, the Lord my shepherd.

David wrote,

> The Lord is my shepherd, I shall not want. He makes
> me to lie down in green pastures; He leads me beside
> the still waters. He restores my soul; He leads me in
> the paths of righteousness for His name's sake. (Ps. 23:
> 1-3)

Our Lord promises that He will take good care of us and lead us in the right path. As a shepherd boy himself, David knew that sheep would only drink from still waters. Like sheep God knows that we can also be pretty scary. But like a good shepherd knows His sheep, our Lord knows us and will not lead us into something we could not handle. However, like sheep we should be able to recognize our master's voice. When their shepherd says, "come" they come, but only in answer to his voice. I remember when I was little and used to play Simon says. Simon says, "take two steps forward" and I would take two steps forward. You lost the game if you went when Simon didn't say so. In our walk with God the world will give us many directions on which way we should go, but we should only move when our Lord says "Go." This requires that we be familiar with our shepherd's voice.

> My sheep listen to my voice; I know them and they fol-
> low me. (John 10:27)

CONTINUAL PRAYER

The key to any relationship, be it family, friend, or spouse, is consistent communication. Communication is also essential to maintaining our relationship with our Lord and Savior Jesus Christ. The importance of prayer is emphasized in both the Old and New Testaments. The Bible tells us that we should be in continual prayer with God, to pray without ceasing (I The. 5:17). Now it would be impossible to go throughout the day with our heads bowed and our eyes closed. I used to think that prayer was always a formal act done at church, before meals, and when I went to bed. Yes, these times should not be neglected, but prayer is also informal. We need to ask for God's guidance as we make various decisions throughout the course of the day. Some decisions may appear to be insignificant at first, yet have very lasting effects on our future. For example, I had an hour commute from where I lived to where I went to school and taught. I would often find myself dialoguing with God about how to handle certain activities that day or just giving Him praise for what He was doing in my life. I know some people driving by must have wondered what in the world I was so happy about. God gave me many chapters and examples for this book on that commute. When I caught on to this, I began to always keep a pen and paper in my car in case I received a word from God. One lesson I shared in the beginning, when God showed me why it doesn't benefit me to try and take shortcuts in my walk with Him.

Prayer does not just involve asking, but praising and receiving as well. The disciples asked Jesus how they should pray. When Jesus gives them an example on how they should pray, His first line was "Our Father in heaven, Hallowed be your name" (Luke 11:2). Before He made any requests He worshipped God for His holiness. He respected God's righteousness. Psalms 100:3-4 states,

> Know that the Lord, He is God; It is He who made us, and not we ourselves; we are His people, the sheep of His pasture. Enter into His gates with thanksgiving and into His courts with praise. Be thankful to Him, and bless His name.

I used to wonder why I would only have temporary success in some endeavors, namely relationships, and then I realized that only what I do for Christ is going to last and everything else is temporal.

Total Obedience. We must surrender our lives to Him, learn of God's ways, pray to Him, but then we must do exactly what He tells us to do. This may seem obvious for Him to be our Lord, but we often only obey a portion of God's word. Yes, we may obey Him in the things that have no value to us, but when God asks us to surrender something of value to Him we act as if it wasn't God speaking. Oftentimes, we think that if we do part of what God has told us to do then He is still pleased. No: we must do exactly what He has told us or we are in disobedience.

God anointed Saul as king and gave Him many victories. When Saul went to fight the Amalekites God told Saul, "Now go, attack the Amalekites and totally destroy everything that belongs to them" (I Sam. 15: 3). So Saul gathered 210,000 men for battle and went to the city of Amelek. Saul and his men destroyed everything, but spared Agag the king and the best of the land. Yet everything that was of no value was totally destroyed. When Samuel confronted Saul, he honestly believed that he had done what was right. However, Samuel assured him that God was not pleased with his disobedience. Samuel asked, "Why did you not obey the Lord? Why did you pounce on the plunder and do evil in the eyes of the Lord?" (I Sam. 15: 20). Yet, Saul states, "I completely destroyed the Amalekites and brought back Agag their king." It was the soldiers who took the best sheep and cattle to sacrifice them to the Lord. Isn't it funny how we always want to blame others for our own disobedience? Samuel explains to Saul that obedience is better than sacrifice and because of his disobedience the Lord rejected him as king of Israel.

Had Saul known the consequences of his actions he probably would have destroyed everything, but he became arrogant and thought that he could do what he wanted because he was king. He also feared displeasing his soldiers more than he feared displeasing God. Many times God will call us to do things that others may not approve of, but if God said it then we need to know that the consequences for our disobedience are always greater than what man can do to us. Yes we will make mistakes and fall occasionally, but if we humble ourselves and repent God will restore us to our rightful position. This was not the first time Saul was disobedient to the word of God. Saul also tried to please the people and disobeyed God by offering up the burnt offering instead of waiting for Samuel to come. When we do not wait on God and try to do things in our own power, God is not pleased. Saul's heart was no longer for God. We must love God with all our heart, all our soul, and all our mind if we are to completely obey His word. Saul's throne was given to David, because his heart longed to please God. Even when

David was disobedient he came to God with a truly repentant heart and God forgave him. If God is going to be Lord in our lives, we must truly desire to please Him by obeying what He has called us to do.

> *Why do you call me ,'Lord, Lord,' and do not what I*
> *say? (Luke 6: 46)*

1. Are there areas where you have been afraid to obey God or speak what is right?

2. How can you begin overcoming fear to obey God fully, without any delay?

Prayer

Lord, I thank you for calling me to be your child and sending your son to die for my sin. I do not deserve the love and kindness you have shown to me. I pray that I live my life in a way that shows you to be Lord of my life. I pray that I do not become to busy to stop and listen to what you have called me to do. I pray that my heart's desire is to do your will and not to please others. Regardless of what others may think, I know that your will is perfect. In order to receive every spiritual blessing you desire for my life, I must be completely obedient to your word. I surrender all to you that you may be glorified in me. Lord, I pray that I die to sin that I may live in Christ. Christ's blood was not shed for me to live in bondage to sin, but to live in freedom. Lord, teach me your ways that I may know your will for my life. Lord, forgive me for times that I was not completely obedient to your word. Lord, I pray I am not led away by my own desires, lust, or pride. Holy spirit strengthen me that I may acknowledge the father in all my ways, so he can direct my path. Amen.

CHAPTER 4

Caution: Potential Friend Ahead

I don't know about you, but I love to be the only one on the highway with a open road before me, not having to worry about maneuvering my way through traffic, just a clear open shot. The only problem with this is that these are the times when I am most tempted to abandon all traffic rules. Though we have freedom in Christ, we also have a responsibility to follow the Word of God. We must realize that yes, we will be blessed; yes we will have God's favor, but it comes at a price. The greater the calling on your life, the greater the sacrifice you will have to make. We must sacrifice all in order to follow Christ.

> *In the same way, any of you who does not give up everything he has cannot be my disciple. (Luke 14:33)*

The Greek translation of the word disciple is *mathetes*, meaning a pupil or learner. However, in the Gospels it also refers to "an adherer who accepts the instruction given to him and makes it his rule of conduct" (KJV). We cannot say that we are followers of Christ if our life does not strive to emulate the life of Christ. Jesus was holy and righteous. He gave up His life to fulfill the will of His father and yet we don't want to give up anything. But it is only after we give up everything that we gain everything. Joseph was exalted to a place of great power, but he was first rejected by his own brothers, lied about by Potiphar's wife, and forgotten in jail. Many of us say "Lord not my will but your will be done" without realizing that His will is not painless and the cross we bear will become heavy. This is why it is so important to remove unnecessary baggage from our lives and focus on serving God. Jesus tells us that on this journey we must make every effort to take the narrow road and only few will find it. If the road you are on is popular and many 'friends' want to follow you, then you may need to question if you're on the right road. It is a true friend that sticks by us when we don't go with the flow. There will also be "frienemies" who we think are our friends but are actually are worst enemies. As we serve God there will be friends, foes, and even family that will be jealous, spiteful, and inconsiderate. In this section we will talk about the importance of choosing the right travel companions on this journey.

CAUTION:

A righteous man is cautious in friendship. Prov. 12:26

Solomon, who was known to be one of the wisest men
of his time, warns about the dangers of wicked and foolish
friendships throughout the entire book of Proverbs. He tells
us to be cautious in choosing whom we call our friends. In
America we use the term "friend" so loosely. People we barely know we introduce as friends, but in other cultures friendships are established over time. In order to be cautious we
must remain prayerful. The Bible warns us not to be anxious
about anything, but to be prayerful about everything. Have
you ever asked God after meeting someone if this is someone that would hinder His will in your life? Many times we
fail to even ask. We meet people and never even consider if
it is God's will to be close with them. Yes, we are to love everyone, but that doesn't mean that we should spend quality
time with everyone. We also see people that we are attracted
to and get carried away in our own lustful desires before we
realize that they were not in God's plan for our life.

I remember I had just met someone for the first time and
they were very nice but something just didn't seem right. I
said "Lord if it is your will for me to become friends with
this person so be it; if not remove them from my life." It
seems that every time we planned to meet for lunch something would happen and I wouldn't be able to make it. Many
times God will give us warnings and allow people to be removed from our lives. Sometimes God will use other people
in our lives to reveal that this is not someone to be closely
associated with. Watch the reactions of others around people
you may consider to be friends. God can use others to show
us things we may have overlooked. Yet still we ignore the

warnings and jump hurdles to be friends with someone that was never intended to be our friend.

We have to be especially cautious, even of those who claim to be our brother or sister in Christ. Paul warns us not to associate closely with a person who claims to be Christians but is sexually immoral or greedy, an idolater or a slanderer, a drunkard or a swindler (I Cor. 5:11). Paul is revealing how we are not to be joined with people who knowingly do wrong and claim to be Christians. They say they are Christian and go to church and may even teach Bible study, but they still practice sexual immorality, or lie and gossip about others, or are drunk every Friday night: not that they occasionally stumble, but that they practice sin religiously. Yes, everyone stumbles but anything we do religiously we do habitually and regularly. It is not that we should seek perfect examples as friends, because no one is perfect. Paul himself does not claim to be without sin and states how all have fallen in sin, but we should not be slaves to sin. Though Paul once persecuted Christians, he was now persecuted himself for righteousness' sake. When God changed him He changed his associations. He began to walk with those he had once hated. When God changes us He changes everything around us, including our friendships. We can no longer be bound to those that were with us before we walked with Christ, unless they decide to change their life as well or if they are our spouse. Paul states how the unbelieving wife will win her husband to Christ just by her conduct. Christ died that we might be free from the bondage of sin, but if we continue to associate with those in sin we may slowly bind ourselves back into sin. Therefore we should seek friendships that will help us to walk in freedom from the bondage of sin.

Let's examine the types of friendships that we are to be cautious of, starting with associations with those who are sexually immoral. Many of us think that Paul is primarily talking about those that are engaging in fornication, but if that were the case he could have just said fornicators. It is possible to be sexually immoral without committing fornication. What about the friends that are always talking about the opposite sex in an immoral way, continually leading your mind away from what it should be focused on? The Bible tells to guard our minds with diligence, but it doesn't help to have friends that make that effort twice as hard. Sexual sin and all sin does not begin with the act, but the thought. The world is already bombarding us with sexually immoral images; we don't need friends in our lives that are adding coal to this fleshly fire.

Now for those friends that are greedy or swindlers: the friends who always want to go somewhere on someone else's dime, who never want to pay for anything and can talk their way out of anything. There is nothing wrong with helping a friend out in hard times, but if they would not be willing to do the same for you, are they true friends? One of the commands that Jesus told us to keep was to love our neighbors as ourselves. If they only love themselves and disregard others are they really your brothers or sisters in Christ? This type of friendship can potentially become burdensome baggage that you should not have to carry. It's one thing to be a good friend and another to be used. Sometimes it can be difficult, but we must remove ourselves from those who are leeching off of others or us. Even if they are not taking up our time, energy, or resources, we may begin to slowly adopt their philosophy that people are simply to be used for our own benefit.

How about friends that are idolaters? You are probably saying to yourselves, "None of my friends worship false gods or graven images!" We often think of the examples used in the Old Testament, but idolatry is simply the worship of a physical object, any object. The other command that Jesus gave us was "Love the Lord your God with all your heart and with all your soul and with all your mind" (Matt. 22: 33). If we love God with all our heart we cannot love the world at the same time. If our friends say they love God then they should not idolize the things of the world such as cars, clothes, or money. God does not mind us having these things, but they should not come before our love for Him. It is the love of money that is the root of all evil, not the money itself. Therefore, we need to be cautious of friends that are constantly talking about money, cars, clothes, or any other materialistic concern. There is a divine purpose for our lives, and that should be our major concern. God tells us to seek His kingdom first and His righteousness, and everything else God will provide (Matt. 6:33). God knows what we need. We must focus on seeking Him above everything else and He will supply our every need.

Paul also states that we should not develop friendships with those that are drunkards. "Oh, they may drink but they never force me to," you say. Well, what about the environment they are placing you in? Many times people use alcohol as an excuse to take part in many other forms of sin. If everyone is drunk except for you, then it's not likely you're in an environment that is going to keep your mind on Christ. No, you may not drink, but they may encourage your participation in other activities that would cause you to sin. A love for revelry or wild partying is also considered to be a sin. By wild partying Paul is not saying it is a sin to have fun; God has given us a life to enjoy. However, parties that promote drunkenness, violence, and sexual promiscuity should not appeal to us as Christians. To be a Christian is to strive to be Christ-like every day, not just on Sundays.

Well, perhaps all your friends aren't sexually immoral, greedy, idolaters, or drunkards, but what about gossipers? Many people think that if they are not participating in the other activities it's okay to talk about those that do, whether or not they even know it's true. Even if it is true, it is not our place to tear down the body by talking about other brothers and sisters behind their backs. We are to hold one another accountable and build each other up. Jesus tells us that if your brother sins against you to go to him in private and show him his fault (Matt 18:15). Nowhere in the verse does it say that you are to go to every other member of the church and reveal his or her faults, before talking to them individually. However, if the sin was committed publicly it often must be corrected publicly. But if you have friends that are constantly criticizing, judging, and condemning others behind their backs you need to remove yourself from them. If they are willing to talk about others to you, what are they telling others about you?

So why is it important that we do not have close associations with the people just described? Because the more we are with them the more we learn of their ways. We are warned in Proverbs 22:24 not to make friends with angry men, because we may find ourselves ensnared in their sin. In the same sense angry men can be substituted with all the other examples given, to include greedy, lustful, gossiping people. We can learn any one of their ways as we continue to be influenced by them. The more we associate with them the stronger their influence is going to be. For example, if you are in an environment consumed with cigarette smoke, though you may not be smoking, once you leave you will carry that smell with you wherever you go. The longer you are there, the stronger the odor will be. Also, if you inhale second-hand smoke consistently you can acquire the same illnesses that a constant smoker would. Think about it: would you put freshly washed clothes with dirty, smelly gym clothes? No, because you know that your clean clothes are likely to start smelling like your gym clothes. Your environment can have the same effect on you, for good or for bad. If you live in sin every day of the week you are likely to take those habits with you to church on Sunday morning. Though you hear the message it cannot take root because your negative environment has a stronger hold on your life. If we are consistently involved in sinful environments eventually we will deal with the same consequences as if we were active participants.

IRON SHARPENS IRON

As iron sharpens iron so one man sharpens another. Pr. 27:17

Some people may have a negative influence on our lives, but others can sharpen our faith. Our faith is strengthened when we have relationships with those of strong faith. As our faith grows stronger others should be strengthened by our faith as well. If you have participated in any competitive activity, you know that the stronger your competitor the better you will be. Though we are not competing with our friends they should still bring out the best in us. If you are an athlete and you continually practice with athletes that do not bring out the best in you, you will never reach your full potential. In whatever it is that we seek to do we are motivated by excellence. I know that part of the reason why I did well in school was because most of my friends were excelling. If I hung around slackers, that is probably what I would have become. We need people around us that will challenge us when we are wrong and that will hold us accountable in our journey for God. In this same chapter of Proverbs verse 6 reads,

Faithful are the wounds of a friend; but the kisses of an enemy are deceitful.

I am so grateful for the words of friends that challenged me to grow deeper in my relationship and walk with God. Though I may have been wounded at the time I was strengthened in the end. If your close friends are always patting you on the back and telling you how great you are, then something is wrong. Either they are deceitful kisses or you have many friends that are unequally yoked. When we are in friendships or relationships with people that are not where we are in Christ, we may have a positive influence on them, but what influence do they have on us? If you always are receiving praise and never being challenged, they may grow but you may become stagnant. I have seen many relationships where one member is really committed to Christ and another is just beginning their walk. As the stronger one tries to encourage the other in their faith, they often become hindered in their own walk. This is not to say that we should not have friendships with those we can encourage, but to say that we must have relationships that strengthen our faith as well.

WHAT A FRIEND WE HAVE IN JESUS

Greater love has no one than this, than to lay down one's life for his friends. (John 15: 13)

We can rest assured when we know what a friend we have in Jesus. People will come and people will go, but no one will ever love us like Jesus does. He was bruised, beaten, and crucified in order for us to be His friend. We show our love for Him when we follow His way and do what He has set out for us to do. In the same chapter Jesus explains that we are not merely servants, because a servant does not know his master's business. However Jesus has made known God's plan for us and we are partakers in His inheritance. When we accept Jesus, we become children of the King, with rights and privileges as His children. Through Jesus we were given direct access to our Heavenly Father, so when we go to our Father and ask for something in Jesus' name He has promised to give it to us. Asking in His name does not mean to just add Jesus' name onto our request. It means that if

Jesus is in us and we are in Him then what we will ask for is in God's will. In Jesus' name there is peace, there is healing, there is sanctification, there is provision, there is joy, and so much more. So as His children we have a right to these things and our Father would love to give them to us, but we must abide in Christ.

The closer our friendship is with Christ the better all our other relationships will be. When we place God first, we will be drawn to others that do the same. However, if we put popularity, self-interest, or anything else first, we will be drawn to others that do the same. God will bring people into your life to encourage you in His will, and as you put Him first you will inspire others. Our other relationships will be enhanced as we grow closer to Christ, because we will begin to love others with the love of Christ. We must consider how Christ loves us even when we have turned away from Him, we will become less upset when people turn away from us. As Jesus was about to give His life the same disciples that promised their devotion to Him had betrayed Him and denied they even knew Him. How could Jesus love us so much, even when we don't show that love back to Him? Because of His great love for His father, He gave His life for us. The closer our relationship is with Christ the easier it will be to forgive, and the easier it will be to love.

As our relationship with God grows the more we will hear from Him and know His will for our lives. When Joseph was alone in jail he had no one to turn to but God, and in that time God taught him many lessons. He learned to become dependent on his relationship with God and not his own ability. Joseph also learned that regardless of the circumstances God never left his side and is able to turn his greatest trial into his greatest blessing. There should not be a day that goes by that we do not turn to God for direction and guidance. Every day we are given is a gift, which is why it is the present. We should not take for granted the gifts God gives to us each day. The closer we are to Him the more we realize that we are nothing without Him.

MAKING JESUS YOUR BEST FRIEND

The more we learn of Him the closer we will be to Him. We often say that we want to have a closer relationship with Christ, but don't know how to accomplish this goal. I had a very good friend as a roommate all throughout college. We have become so close that we could just look at each other and each know what the other is thinking. However, it was not this way when we first met. Only after many years and experiences together did this relationship grow. The same philosophy applies to our relationship to Christ. We have to share our life with Him and invite Him on our journey. Being the gentleman that He is He will not force His way in and just start changing our lives. He will knock on the door of our heart and we must choose to invite Him in. When we invite Jesus to take this journey with us we will find that we cannot go to places we used to go or associate with certain people. We will not feel comfortable bringing Jesus into sin and darkness. What association can light have with darkness? None; they cannot both exist simultaneously. Jesus reveals to us that when we walk by the light of day we will not stumble, but if we walk in darkness we will. We must choose one or the other, and if we choose Jesus we choose to walk in the light.

Constant awareness of His presence. We need to be aware of God's presence wherever we go, not just in church. The Word tells us that we are to continually be prayerful, giving thanks in all circumstances. You may start the day in prayer, but we must desire His presence and guidance everywhere we go. On my way to work I can give praise to God with inspirational music, but also pray that He will lead me and guide me, that He give me wisdom and patience as I drive and protect me from danger. I think I have had many of my most productive talks with God on my way to work or school. You may be in a stressful situation at work and just say a silent prayer for God to strengthen you. We don't have to wait until Sunday morning; we can call on God right then and there. When we seek Him early He gives us the patience and endurance to walk in righteousness. When we don't seek Him early we find ourselves asking for forgiveness when we impatiently react to situations.

> *I love those who love me, and those who seek me early will find me. (Prov. 8:17)*

We must learn to be proactive and not reactive. If we seek Him before we encounter a stressful or emotional situation He will have already given us what we need to make it through the trial. It is a continual dialogue that we are having with Jesus. In the morning we thank God for giving us what we need to do His will on this day. In the afternoon we may need to be renewed and strengthened. In the evening we can praise Him for carrying us through. There is not an hour in

the day when God is not actively involved in our lives and
we need to be aware of his presence. In His presence we will
find peace and fullness of joy (Ps. 16:11).

Make yourself available to Him. The more time we spend
with Him the more He will reveal Himself to us, as well as
reveal our own weaknesses. One thing about having a good
friend is that they will hold you accountable. There have
been many times, whether in prayer, in worship, or in His
word that Jesus would reveal where I need to grow in Him.
God cannot reveal things to us if we never take the time to
listen. It's important that we read our Bible and pray, but just
as important that we listen. There should be time in your day
or throughout the day when you can spend time alone with
God. I was blessed to have gone to college near the beach.
There were days when I would go to the beach and look at
the ocean and, as the waves would roll out and come back
in, God could speak to me. Now that I'm in Georgia, I may
just look out at the trees and hear from God. For me, something about being in nature, without telephones, emails, or
other distractions, allows me to have more intimacy in my
talk with God. Nature also reveals how small any problem of
ours really is to the Creator of the universe. If God can work
everything out in nature so perfectly that every bird, every
tree, every ocean is maintained, can He not work out the seasons of our lives. Whether we are outside or inside we need
to be in a place where we can be alone with God. Whether
we have to resort to a bathroom or a closet to be alone with
God; wherever it is, whenever it is, make the time.

Have you ever had friends that are always asking for
your opinion, but never listen to the advice that is given?

You may be trying to have a serious conversation with them and they are watching television or thinking about something else and not listening to what you have to say. It can be very frustrating. I hope Jesus isn't as easily frustrated, as we constantly ask for His advice but never give Him the chance to answer, and when He does we don't listen. We are too busy talking to someone else, finishing this or that, or telling God what He should be doing. Jesus tells us that we show that we are His friend when we listen to what He has to say and obey him.

Make it a habit to follow His directions. The more we follow Him the less we will ask for His direction. We talked earlier about how, when we continue to take the same way home, we think less about the directions and just follow them unconsciously. We need to be so close to God that His spirit begins to lead us in everything that we do, even when we are not consciously asking for His help. Throughout my life my mom has given me many instructions, and as I grew older I began to follow many instructions without even thinking about it. For example, I always grab a jacket or sweater "just in case." I suppose I think of the times when I didn't follow her advice and nearly froze to death. I can be in situations where I just know what my mom would say, without even asking. The more we learn of Christ and follow His directions, the less confused we will be as we encounter various situations. We will be in situations and a scripture will come to mind or the Holy Spirit will just show us what God's will is, but whether or not we follow His guidance is up to us.

1. Are your friends sharpening your iron or weakening your faith?

2. How can you begin strengthening your relationship with Christ?

Prayer

My Father, I thank you for loving me so much that you would not call me servant, but your friend. I thank you Jesus for knocking on the door of my heart. From this day on, I will invite you in to take this journey with me. Show me your will and I will do it. Reveal to me the people that will encourage me in my faith, as well as those that will lead me away from the straight and narrow path you have given. I pray that I will not allow people that are sexually immoral, idolaters, swindlers, drunkards, or gossipers to have influence on your plan for my life. I choose to walk with you and therefore I must walk in light and not in darkness. Let me resist every temptation to walk in darkness. Lord, I need your direction in my life and I pray I am never too busy to spend time with you. The more time I make for you the less time I will waist in my life. I choose now to walk by your spirit and not by my flesh. I choose now to walk by faith and not by sight. I choose now to walk in righteousness and not in wickedness. Amen.

CHAPTER 5

Driving in the Dark

IS THE PRICE RIGHT?

Have you ever watched a game show where the contestant is asked to pick one of three doors? They may have won a prize already, and they can walk away or they could go for more and choose a prize behind door number 1, 2, or 3. They decide they will risk it all and try for a bigger prize, but which door will it be? Maybe door number 1 will have a shiny new car waiting for them, or perhaps door number 3. The pressure is on and they finally blurt out "Door number 3!" The audience looks on with anticipation of what they will see behind door number 3. Finally the moment they have been waiting for has come; the door is opened and what's behind the door is not shiny or new, but simply a goat. The contestant's face dramatically changes from excitement and anticipation to disappointment and disgust. The game show host states, "Ahh, that's too bad, but we have some great consolation prizes for you!"

Many times as Christians we also find ourselves disappointed with what the world has to offer. Though we have the greatest prize in Christ, we trade it all in and get nothing in return. Jesus tells us, "What good is it to gain the whole world and lose your soul?" (Matt. 16:26) When Satan tempted Jesus, he took Him up to a high mountain and promised to give Him all the kingdoms of the world and their splendor if He would bow down and worship him. But Jesus knew who He was and who His Father was. When we are tempted to go away from what God has for us, the decision to choose the Lord's way is easier when you know who you are and who your Father is. We serve a God that created the heavens and the earth and it all belongs to Him and Him alone. Psalms 50 reveals how every creature, every mountain, the entire world and everything that is in it belongs to our God. What a privilege it is to be a child of the King!

Walking in Darkness

Without God in our lives we would constantly make decisions based on greed, lust, and pride ending up worse off each time. Without God's direction and guidance even the simplest task can be difficult. Why? Because we have no light, if Jesus is the light of the world, then without Him we live in darkness. Imagine a world with no sunshine to bring us warmth, no moon to lead us at night, no stars to give us direction. That is our life without Jesus- cold, confusing, and chaotic.

When I was visiting my brother in Seattle, God revealed to me what life was like without Him as my light. My brother lived in a rural area of Washington, up a mountain, with no lights. I was sleeping one night and had to get up for some reason. It was pitch black. I couldn't even see my hand directly in front of my face. This was my first visit there and I was not familiar with my surroundings. If you've ever woken up in an unfamiliar place, you know it can be a little scary. I inched my way towards what I thought was the door with my hands in front of me. I was confronted with a wall. Feeling my way down the wall, I finally made it to the bedroom door.

When I woke up the next morning I began to think how lost I would be without Christ in my life. Yes, I may reach some minor goals, but even they would have been so much easier with God's light leading the way. Even God, the Creator of the Universe, chose to work by light. After God had created the heavens and the earth, before He separated the waters, formed the land, or made any living thing He commanded "Let there be light" (Gen. 1:3). Jesus also chose to walk in light. When the disciples feared for Jesus' life, He told them, "A man who walks by day will not stumble." Yet we choose to walk in darkness. We tell the Lord "One day I will follow your way, but today I'd rather stumble in darkness for now." We wonder why everything seems to always go wrong when oftentimes it's because we did not allow the Lord to be our light.

Jesus came to be our Savior. If a father looked down and saw his child running as fast as she could, unaware that eventually she was going to run full force into a brick wall, would he not want to save them? Our Father has His hand extended toward us, but we must take hold of it, with all our might and all our strength. Christ came that He might save us from a life of darkness and confusion by bringing us into His marvelous light.

God is light and in Him is no darkness at all. If we say
we have fellowship with Him, and walk in darkness, we
lie and do not practice the truth.(I John 1:5-6)

I don't know about you, but I don't want to live a lie.
So how do we know if we are walking in light or in darkness? We must first take time to examine our actions and
ask, "Where is our spirit or our flesh leading us?" The works
of the flesh are adultery, fornication, uncleanness, and las-
civiousness (Gal. 5:19, KJV). The King James version states
that these works are manifest, meaning open, blatant, done
without shame. So if we examine our actions they should be
easily revealed. If they are done openly, we might not even
consider them to be sins. Regardless of how accepted they
may be from the world's point of view, it's still sin.

The first two works are pretty self explanatory, but another version mentions them as "sexual immorality" (NIV),
which includes more than just fornication and adultery.
You can technically be a virgin or abstinent and be living
in sexual immorality. The Bible tells us how important our
eyes are in keeping the rest of our body pure. Jesus stated,
"The eye is the lamp of the body. If your eyes are good, your
whole body will be full of light. But if your eyes are bad,
your whole body will be full of darkness" (Matt 6:22-23).
What movies are you watching? The enemy is persistently
seeking to fill our minds with sexual images. We can't just
sit idly in front of t.v. or go to a movie because everyone else
goes. We need to stop and think "Is this movie beneficial to
God's purpose in my life?" It doesn't just stop with movies
or t.v.: the enemy is steadily gaining more and more access

in magazines, in music, and on the internet. The word tells to guard our minds with all diligence. Why? Because when the devil can fill our mind with anything contrary to the word of God, he can distract us from fulfilling God's purpose in our lives. All these images will begin to affect how you look at members of the opposite sex. Do you look at them as your brother or sister in Christ or as your next fling? No, it's not a sin to notice that someone is attractive, but Christ tells us that when we even look at some in lust we have already committed adultery in our hearts. We must always be on guard and pray that we will recognize when the enemy is tempting us and then remove ourselves from the situation.

The next two sins Paul describes might also be misinterpreted. When "uncleanness" is mentioned it is not so much a concern for your outward appearance, but of the impurity of one's heart. Though we may put on a good show and appear holy and righteous in our Sunday best, God is not impressed. God states in I Sam. 16:7,

> But the Lord said to Samuel, "Do not look at his appearance or at his physical stature, because I have rejected him. For he Lord does not see as man sees; for man looks at the outward appearance, but the Lord looks at the heart."

Millions of dollars are spent each year on improving outward appearances. It is a good thing to take care of ourselves and eat nutritiously, but what good is that healthy body to God if we only use it for sin? We should take care of ourselves so that we can do God's will without hindrance. Our body is to be a temple for the Living God; yes it should look presentable, but more importantly when you go inside it should reflect God's holiness. Though people may only judge our outward appearances, God judges us by our hearts. When God chose David to be anointed King, he may have appeared to be the weakest of his brothers in stature, but he had the greatest heart to serve God. Just as God allowed Samuel to see the character of David and his brothers, God will reveal our true character to others as well. Not that we should live for man's approval, but people are always watching. Even those that don't believe in God can look at us and say, "How can you do that, aren't you supposed to be a Christian?" So before others question us, we should examine ourselves and know whether we are revealing light or darkness.

Paul continues to mention other works of the flesh that should be avoided, such as idolatry and witchcraft. Idolatry is merely the worship of a physical object and witchcraft is described as the practice of magic arts and also the use of drugs and magical potions. Our society is slowly becoming more and more accepting of both idolatry and witchcraft. Popular television shows, movies, and books are portraying witches, sorcerers, and charmers in a positive light. Do not be deceived by the enemy: these portrayals are in direct contradiction to the Word of God and we should not support such shows, books, or movies as Christians. God has given us the answer to all our questions in his word. Therefore, we should not seek understanding through astrological signs, zodiac signs, or psychics. We should not place our faith in anything or anyone else besides Jesus Christ.

Though idolatry and witchcraft are more openly rejected, other works of the flesh are still blatantly practiced by

Christians, such as hatred, jealousy, and emulation. Jesus told us that the greatest commandment is to love our neighbor as ourselves: He never promised that they would love us back. Yet while we were sinners Jesus gave His life for us not because we deserved salvation, but because of His awesome love for us. We should love others in the same way: not in and of ourselves, but because of Jesus' love in us. Jesus asks "How can we say we love our father in heaven, whom we have not seen; yet hate our brother or sister we see daily?" It amazes me how others are so quick degrade other brothers and sisters in Christ, other churches or pastors; yet when Jesus found the women about to be stoned for committing adultery He didn't condemn her and protected her from the condemnation of others. He simply stated to her, in private, "Go and sin no more." If we first love God more than anything, it makes it easier to love everyone else. We should want the very best for others, knowing that our Father will supply all our needs according to His riches and glory, which are endless. If we strive to be like Christ we will not desire to emulate any other person.

Paul concludes his list of fleshly works by mentioning drunkenness and revelry. Anything can hinder our walk with God when done in excess or out of the will of God. Just as God has given us food to nourish our bodies, we should not eat in such excess that God would not be glorified. We must live our lives on purpose, realizing that everything we do serves a purpose and that purpose should help us to fulfill God's will in our lives. We must continually examine ourselves and ask the Holy Spirit to reveal to us any action that hinders our walk with God. Jesus told His disciples before they took communion,

> *But let a man examine himself, and so let him eat of the bread and drink of the cup. For he who eats and drinks in an unworthy manner eats and drinks judgment to himself, not discerning the Lord's body. (I Cor. 11:28-29)*

Instead of reacting to God's judgment of our sin, we need to be proactive in repenting of our sin before it is able to consume us.

LIVING IN THE LIGHT

Paul warns us that the sinful nature is in constant battle with our spiritual nature and that we must live by the spirit. Though we desire to do good the flesh seeks to do evil. However, "Those controlled by the sinful nature cannot please God" (Rom. 8:8). If we sow seeds into the sinful nature we will reap the consequences of that sin: however, if we sow seeds into our spiritual nature we reap the benefits as children of God. After understanding what seeds of sin should not be sown in our life, we must address what seeds should be sown in our life. Every time we go to church, pray, worship, or fast, we are sowing seeds that will produce fruit of the spirit. Paul reveals the works of the flesh, and then he reveals the fruit of the spirit as love, joy, peace, patience, kindness, goodness, faithfulness, gentleness and self-control (Gal. 5:22-23). If we are living in the light then such fruit should be evident in our lives. Our minds should be set not on what the flesh desires, but on what the spirit desires. How do we know we see an apple tree? We recognize it because we recognize the apples it produces. The apple tree started out as just a small apple seed that was sown. If an apple seed were planted, we would not expect an orange tree to grow from that seed. In the same manner, we should display the fruit of the spirit if we are sowing seeds of the spirit and not of the flesh. Jesus tells the disciples that you will recognize false prophets not by their appearance, for they will be as wolves dressed in sheep's clothing, but by the fruit they produce:

> A good tree cannot bear bad fruit, and a bad tree cannot bear good fruit. Every tree that does not bear good fruit is cut down and thrown into the fire. Thus, by their fruit you will recognize them. (Matt. 7: 18-20, NIV)

Love is the first fruit that should be seen on our tree. When Jesus was asked which commandment was the most important, he stated; "Love the Lord your God with all your heart and with all your soul and with all your mind. This is the first and greatest commandment" (Matt 22:37-38). If we place God as number one in our lives, we will not walk in the flesh. Instead of concentrating so much on what we should not be doing, if we put our love for God first, everything else will fall into place. Jesus told the Pharisee that the second greatest commandment was to "Love your neighbor as yourself." If we truly love others as ourselves it would be impossible to be envious or jealous of our brothers and sisters because we would want the very best for them. Their joy would be our joy, and their sorrow our sorrow.

It is difficult to love others when you hate yourself. You must realize, as David did (Ps. 139:14), that God fearfully and wonderfully made you and He cannot make mistakes. Regardless of what others may have fed into your spirit, you must know that God has a purpose and plan for your life. You are not here by accident and the world would lose something valuable if you were not in it. When we know who we are in Christ Jesus and who are Father is we can love others with the love of Christ. We will not feed off their defeat or try to place a stumbling block in their path because we are one in the Body of Christ. If the eye suffers the whole body suffers; all parts of the body are valuable and vital to the operation of the body as a whole.

Other fruits that should be seen on our tree are joy and peace. People should know that we are Christians by the joy that we possess. They should be thinking, "I don't know how he/she could be so joyful and peaceful in a time like this." We should be able to say; "I don't know either, if it weren't for Jesus." We should have joy and peace in the midst of trials because we know that our God will never leave us or forsake us. Also, we know that God desires to give the very best to his children, if we only obey Him. We can look at the situation and know that it does not affect our destination. What God has for us it is for us, and no weapon shall prosper against it. Isaiah 55 reveals that whatever God says must come to pass, and His word can never return to Him void. We should not doubt what God has said He would do in our lives, we can rest assure that it will come to pass.

No matter what occurs in life, when we think of God's goodness and faithfulness to us we have reason to be joyful and at peace that He will not change. In the Old Testament you often find that every time God delivered His people from something they would bring a remnant of that act to strengthen their faith and their children's faith in the future. For example, when they crossed the Jordan they carried out twelve stones from the middle of the Jordan. When God allows us to cross over our Jordan we need to write it down or do something that will remind us in the future that God is determined to bring us out. When we think on what He has done we can rejoice in the God of our salvation. Why should we worry about tomorrow when we see how good God is today? Jesus tells us in Matt. 6, not to worry about our lives. The birds never worry about how they will be fed and God provides for them daily. Look how beautiful the flowers of the field are clothed. Yet God cares for us much more than them, so how much more will he provide for us? If you only

> Seek first the kingdom of God and His righteousness, and all these things shall be added to you. Therefore do not worry about tomorrow, for tomorrow will worry about its own things. (Matt. 6:33-34)

Patience should also be seen on our tree of life. All the fruits of the spirit compliment one another. When we do not allow circumstances to affect our joy or peace, it is easier to wait patiently on the Lord. However, if we allow worry to consume our thoughts we will become anxious and fearful. Philippians 4 is always a good chapter to read whenever we may feel anxious. It reads,

Be anxious for nothing, but in everything by prayer and supplication, with thanksgiving, let your requests be known to God; and the peace of God, which surpasses all understanding, will guard your hearts and minds through Christ Jesus. (Phil. 4:6-7)

When we take all our requests to God we only have peace if we leave them there. Many of us tell God our requests and just as He is about to impact the situation for our good, we take it back in our impatience. This is why it is impossible to please God without faith. We must have faith that He will do whatever it is we ask in Jesus Christ. When we say "Lord not my will but your will be done," we surrender all control over the situation. That is not an easy thing to do, but it becomes easier once we realize that every time we try to manipulate the situation ourselves we end up moving farther and farther from God's will. I know I am guilty of believing that I could do everything on my own, but then I came to the realization that even if I could, God could do it so much better. Jesus reveals how God loves to provide His children with good gifts. He states, "If you, then, being evil, know how to give good gifs to your children, how much more will you Father in heaven give good things to those who ask Him!" (Matt. 7: 11) Yet, we are too proud to even ask. Some of us are born with this independence and some use it as a defense mechanism to hide weakness. When I was a baby I didn't even want my mother to feed me, though I would have received more food with her help; I was determined to do it myself. It is the same in life; we must not allow pride or independence to hinder our dependence on God. Yes, we may be able to accomplish great things on our own, but they could be so much greater when we allow God to take control.

Kindness, goodness, and gentleness should also be evident in our lives. It is easier to display these qualities when we already have obtained fruits of love, joy, peace, and patience. It is difficult to be kind to someone you hate. It is also difficult to display gentleness when we are impatient. Impatience leads right into anger and sometimes can become rage. However, when we realize that God is in control of the situation it so much easier to be kind and loving toward someone, even when they are spiteful towards you. How so? Because we place our faith in God and not in people, nothing they say or do can affect what God has for us. So why lose our future blessing by allowing ourselves to be consumed with anger, fear, or doubt? God said that He would make our enemies our footstools, not for us to crush them, but for them to be a blessing to us. The very person that you may be praying for God to remove from your life might be the same person He uses to open the door to a blessing greater than you could have ever conceived.

> But without faith it is impossible to please Him, for he who comes to God must believe that He is a rewarder of those who diligently seek Him. (Heb. 11:6)

Faithfulness is also a fruit that should be evident on our tree. It was only by faith that Joshua was able to lead the people across the Jordan River without fear. The only way we will be able to cross our Jordan, with joy, peace, and love, is to know that our God is in total control and He will reward those that seek Him diligently. Regardless of how the enemy tries to shake our faith and cause us to doubt God's ability, we must be able to stand on God's word. You see the enemy knows the good things God has in store for us and, quite honestly, he is jealous that he will never receive them again. So if the enemy can cause us to be anxious and fearful our faith can be shaken. However, we must immerse ourselves in God word so that he will not be able to shake our faith. When we read II Timothy, we understand that fear is contrary to the will of God in our lives.

> For God has not given us the spirit of fear; but of power, and of love, and of a sound mind.(II Tim. 1:7)

We should not let our guard down and let all kinds of thoughts enter our mind, such as thoughts of doubt, despair, and hopelessness. If faith is the substance of things hoped for and the evidence of things unseen (Heb. 11:1), then the situation does not require faith if we know how things are going to work out. God knew every need we would ever have before we were even born. God told Jeremiah,

> Before I formed you in the womb, I knew you, before you were born I set you apart; I appointed you as a prophet to the nations.(Jer. 1:5)

David rejoiced when he realized that God ordained his days before they came into existence (Ps. 139: 16). When we realize that God has prepared to meet every need we will ever have, why should we lose faith? All throughout the Bible, and particularly in Joshua, God reminds us to not fear, but to be strong and courageous. We can be strong in faith and courageous in our actions when we allow God to lead us.

Lastly, our lives should display self-control. Though we may not have control over some situations or circumstances, we should display self-control within any situation. All the fruits of the spirit work in accordance with one another. The peace of God gives patience and patience adds to self-control, which allows us to limit what we say or do. Through faith we know that God will always provide a way of escape and will not allow us to be tempted beyond what we can bear. So if we say "I simply can't stop cursing, smoking, fornicating, drinking, gossiping," we lie and we have no faith.

We can do all things through Christ that strengthens us (Phil. 4:13). By the power of the Holy Spirit we can come against any sin in our life. God would not convict us of something that He is not prepared to correct, but we have to let Him. Oftentimes, it is not that we cannot overcome whatever sin is in our lives; it is that we choose not to live without it. Most addictions or destructive habits, though damaging spiritually and sometimes physically, are serving a purpose in our lives: perhaps to help us cope with a troubled childhood, abuse, and/or a negative self-image. But God will not only ease the pain, He will heal us of our pain and fill the emptiness with His loving spirit. When we allow God to fulfill that need it is easier to walk in self-control and realize that this sin is only holding us back from receiving God's very best in our lives. When we study God's word, we become more knowledgeable of who we are in Christ Jesus, and once we receive this knowledge we are held accountable to act accordingly. We cannot tell God that we didn't know, because it was revealed in His word. Once we are aware of how we should live it is up to us to choose to walk in the light.

> *For you were once in darkness, but now you are light in the Lord. Live as children of light. (Eph. 5:8)*

1. What fruit(s) of the spirit does your life reveal?
2. What fruit(s) of the spirit do you need to reveal more?

Prayer

Lord Jesus, I realize that you came down from heaven, died on the cross and rose again that I might live a sanctified life. Lord, I pray that you not only save me from this world of sin, but that you sanctify me to do your will. My flesh is struggling with my spirit and I pray that my spirit is strengthened by the power of your Holy Spirit. I pray that you are glorified in my life and that people will know I am a child of God by the fruits I display. Help me to avoid the works of the flesh, because I know I will not inherit your kingdom if I live by my sinful nature. Your death released me from the chains of these sins and I will not allow the enemy to lead me back into bondage. I pray that I grow stronger in love, joy, peace, patience, kindness, faithfulness, and self-control. Lord, I know that when I strive to attain these fruits in my life, you can use me more fully to do your will. I pray that I shake off every weight that hinders my walk in you. Lord your word is a light unto my feet and I know you will never lead me astray. Forgive me of my sins and by your power I will not return to them. I thank you Father for your grace, mercy, and unconditional love in my life. Amen.

CHAPTER 6

Good, Better, Best

When I was just a little girl, my mother shared with me a saying that my great grandmother always favored: "Good, better, best, never let it rest until your good is better and your better is best." My mother was never satisfied with a half-hearted effort and always pushed me to do my personal best. It may not be as good as Johnny or Susan's best, but it was my very best.

The same goal should prove true in our relationship with God. We should seek God's very best for our lives. Yet, many times we settle for a mediocre relationship with God and bear little fruit. God said that not only has He given us life, He has given it to us abundantly. When we abide in Him and He in us, **then** we can ask and have no doubt that God will supply. If we are abiding in Him, we are not seeking our own will, but the will of the Father. We pray to the Lord that He be glorified in our lives, not realizing that we must die to our flesh for Him to be glorified. Jesus prayed to the father, "I have brought you glory on earth by completing the work you gave me to do" (John 17:4). Jesus submitted to the Father's will unto death, that He would be resurrected and reveal God's glory magnificently. What work has the Father given you to do? Has it been completed? Each day we should strive to accomplish what God has set out for us to do that day. We want to receive the Father's best, but it will require that we not just seek to do what is good, but what is best. God may require things of you that you don't see Him requiring of anyone else; that is because it is to fulfill His calling on your life alone. The enemy will try to put up distractions and barriers to prevent us from completing the work God has called us to do and our own flesh will struggle against us, but we can do all things in Christ that strengthens us. For Christ had to deny the desires of His flesh and resist every hindrance the enemy used in order that God receive the glory in His life.

> Everything is permissible – but not everything is beneficial. Everything is permissible – but not everything is constructive. (I Cor. 10: 23, NIV)

God does not force us to choose what is best for our lives. He gives us free will to make decisions on a daily basis. We are not puppets and God the great puppeteer in this stage called life. He gives us choices and we must be led by the spirit to choose what is best. God may allow us to form relationships, but we must ask: Is this really God's best? *Is this relationship allowing me to become the person God has called me to be?* "Everything is permissible – but not everything is constructive" (I Cor. 10:23). To construct is to build or to make. We must ask *what is this relationship or activity building in me? Is it making me more like Christ?* If it's not then we must pray if it is something we need to let go. There are times when

God will allow us to experience something for a brief season. For whatever reason He placed us in a particular job, church, relationship and then when His will is done He calls us out of that season. What used to be best is now hindering our growth. As difficult as it is to walk away, we must realize that we will never attain God's best if we don't. God promised to make Abraham a great nation, but he first had to walk away from everything, be willing to sacrifice his most beloved possessions, and remain faithful to God's call.

We must realize that in order to attain God's very best it would be to our benefit if we seek the Father's wisdom in all our decisions. Jesus tells us that whatever we ask in His name will be given to us (John 16:24). He promises us that our joy will be complete. It is not our Father's will for us to live miserable lives. If we know that we are children of the king and that He promised to supply all of our need according to His riches and glory, there is no reason why we should feel sorry for ourselves. Jesus reminds us not to worry about what we will eat or what we will wear.

> Look at the birds of the air; they do not sow or reap or store away in barns, and yet your heavenly Father feeds them. Are you not more valuable than they? (Matt. 6:26)

All of this to say that whatever it is that God has called you to do, He will be sure to supply everything you need to accomplish that goal. Many of us go to schools, take jobs, and even form relationships that are not according to God's divine will in our lives. Oftentimes, we make these decisions in fear and impatience. We allow the world to dictate what we should do instead of waiting for the Lord's deliverance, which was shown in the life of Saul. Just like Saul, God will permit someone else to take on the work, the opportunity, the relationship that He had destined for us to have. I don't know about you, but I don't want to make it to heaven and find out that there was so much more that God wanted to do in my life and I let the world talk me out of attaining my best -- or worse yet, that I talked myself out of striving harder and reaching further. Anything worth having is not going to be easily attained. God will have to prepare us to walk in a higher level of favor and blessing, as He prepared Joseph and David. God revealed the great things He would do in their lives at a young age, but it wasn't until they had overcome many obstacles that they walked in the fullness of that blessing. What if Joseph had given up in jail and allowed his circumstances to dictate how far he would go? What if he had lost his temper and lashed out at Pharoah, when his wife wrongfully accused him of rape? Or what if he would have allowed his flesh to give in to his wife's advances? How would it have affected how God would later be glorified in his life? Everything Joseph desired was given to him abundantly, but only after his faith had been tested. Not every piece of coal will be able to withstand the pressure it takes to become a diamond. Regardless of what others might say, withstand the test knowing that your Father knows your way and will bless you in the end. As Job stated,

> But he knows the way that I take; when he has tested
> me, I will come forth as gold. (Job 23:10)

THE HIGH CALLING

One of the most prolific writers in the Bible, Paul, would not settle for mediocrity in his relationship with God. Paul realized that in order to walk in the divine will of God for his life, he must be willing to sacrifice. To receive God's very best for our lives we must be willing to give God our best. Great men and women in the Bible that attained great success also endured great sacrifices. Abraham had to leave his native land and later be willing to sacrifice his only son. Joseph also was forced to leave his family and then be wrongfully accused of rape. Ruth lost her husband and then chose to stay with Naomi and forsake her family, friends, and former customs. Paul began running with the crowd he once persecuted, so his former friends became his persecutors. Yet, Paul stated that everything he lost was nothing to the great gift of knowing Christ Jesus as his Lord (Phil. 3: 8). God will also call us to new places, new jobs, new churches, and new relationships in order that we might attain his best will for our lives. Though these things may have been good, God desires our best. This is why it is so important that we place nothing and no one before our relationship with God. If we do we will choose to stay committed to them and not to what God may call us to do. If He says go, we must go. If He says stay, we must stay. If He says wait, we must wait. What He calls us to may not make sense to others, but if we know that God said it then we must follow Him. How do we know if God said it? What He calls us to will always bring us closer to him and allow us to grow spiritually. God never tempts us to sin (Jam. 1: 13): He tests our faith, not our flesh. When we

walk in God's perfect plan for our lives, He will open doors
and give us favor greater than we ever imagined. However,
we must be willing to share in Christ's sufferings and perse-
vere when our faith is tested.

> *These have come so that your faith of greater worth than*
> *gold, which perishes Even though refined by fire – may*
> *be proven genuine and may result in praise, glory and*
> *honor when Jesus Christ is revealed. (I Pet. 1: 7, NIV)*

Unlike many of us, Paul stated that not only did he want
to "know Christ and the power of his resurrection," but also
the "fellowship of sharing in His sufferings, becoming con-
formed to His death..." (Phil. 3: 10). We all are excited about
receiving the power of God in our lives, but oftentimes that
power is the result of pain. Paul was even excited about the
test, knowing that in the end he would be more like Christ.
After we have shared in Christ sufferings and endured ridicule and rejection, we have power to be able to minister to
others who are going through what God allowed us to overcome. God allows our test to become our testimony.

In order for us to overcome our test we must not dwell
in the past, but continue to strive for higher heights in Christ
Jesus. We must not forget God's faithfulness to us in the past,
but we should be just as excited about what God is doing in
our lives right now. Each day we should grow just a little bit
closer to what God has called us to be in Christ. Paul stated,

> *Brethren, I count not myself to have apprehended: but*
> *this one thing I do, forgetting those things which are*
> *behind, and reaching forth unto those this things which*

*are before, I press toward the mark for the prize of the
high calling of God in Christ Jesus. (KJV, Phil. 3: 13-
14)*

We often pray to God to remove every hardship, but if He did we would never grow in Christ. As babies we need to feel our mother's presence, and if they left us for a moment we would cry and long for them to come back. Eventually, they would have to let us cry a while and learn that things would be okay even when they weren't right there. If they continued to hold us every minute of the day, we would form an unhealthy attachment that would later hinder us. Our heavenly Father also allows us to grow spiritually as we overcome obstacles in our life. He is with us in the storm, but we must still walk on our own. We may not always feel Him like we did as babes in Christ, but He is still right there. As Peter walked on the water toward Jesus, we too must continue to walk by faith and not by sight.

ATTAINING GOD'S BEST

*Eye has not seen, no ear heard,
Nor have entered into the heart of man
The things which God has prepared for those who love
Him. (I Cor. 2: 9)*

Expect God's Best. Why do we put limitations on what God can do in our lives? We will never receive God's best for our lives when we don't think that it is possible. We need to realize that what God has in store for us is so much greater than what we could have ever imagined. No mind has even thought of what God has for those who love Him. So don't be afraid when God puts something on your heart that you have never seen done before. That's what God does: He creates something from nothing. He is the Creator and whatever He speaks must come to pass. God spoke the world into existence. Everything He told you He would do for you must take place, for His word must accomplish what it set out to do. God states in Isaiah that as the rain does not return without watering the earth and creating new life, "so is my word that goes out from my mouth: It will not return to me empty, but will accomplish what I desire and achieve the purpose for which I sent it" (Isa. 55: 11). As we are created in His image we must speak our dreams into existence, even if everyone you know says you're crazy. You must not curse yourself, by saying that you can't do something or that you are not qualified. In our weakness, He is made strong. You may not be qualified on your own, but you can do all things through Christ that strengthens you (Phil. 4:13). God opens a door and when He does, we are afraid to walk through. God will never fail us, but we must not fail God. Don't let the enemy talk you out of your blessing. Don't be overly confident in your own abilities, but be convinced that if God has called you to something He is faithful to complete His work in you.

Our God is the God of impossibility. He uses the most unlikely people to do extraordinary tasks. Samuel almost chose David's brother because of his appearance, but the Lord chose David because of his heart to serve. That is our greatest strength. When we desire to please God above anything else, He will give us the desires of our hearts. It is impossible to please God without faith. David did not doubt that God would give him the victory against Goliath. We need to stand up against what may appear as giants in our lives and claim our victory in Christ Jesus. Jesus tells us that if we only have faith the size of a mustard seed, which is only a little bigger than the period at the end of this sentence, we can move mountains.

> For as the heavens are higher than the earth, so are My ways higher than your ways and My thoughts higher than your thoughts. (Isa. 55: 9)

We must pray for God to allow us to see things through His eyes and not our own. However, it requires a great deal of faith for us to see what may seem to be impossible as an opportunity for God to be glorified in our lives. God may allow us to have our back against the wall, with no one to turn to, in order to show us that He is our deliverer. As Americans we have been so blessed that our faith is often hindered. Instead of depending on God we depend on our own wealth, other people, or the government to supply our needs. Yet, God has called us to walk by faith and not by sight. Our Christian brothers and sisters in Africa and China risk their lives to practice the faith we take for granted. We let the slightest inconvenience prevent us from going to church or bible study, witnessing to others, or praising God, while they pray for such opportunities. I pray that God give me the faith of biblical days, not today's faith. I want faith to realize that God is still God even when I don't feel Him or see any evidence of Him.

Job knew he was blessed by God and was upright and holy in all his ways. However, when God allowed him to be stripped of his wealth, lose his sons and daughters, be cursed by friends as well as his own wife, he still worshipped God. After losing his wealth and his children Job stated:

"The Lord gave and the Lord has taken away; may the name of the Lord be praised" (Job 1:21). If God never did another thing for us would we still bless him? After losing our job, our child, our spouse, would we still give God praise? This is why Jesus told the disciples that if you consider your family more than God, you are not fit to serve. The disciples had to trust God daily to provide for their needs. In order for God to use us greatly, He has to know that He can trust us in good times and in bad. When you don't have the money to lend and you give it to your brother in need that's when it matters most. When you are hungry and you give your food to someone in need, God knows that He can trust you to be a blessing even when you are not blessed. Like Job, God gave him twice as much as he had before, because of his faithfulness to trust God in the valley, not just on the mountaintop.

Step out on faith. There are visions unrealized and dreams unfilled because we are scared to take the first step and then keep on stepping. Whatever it is that is preventing us from fulfilling the work God has for us to do must be addressed. If it is fear of losing everything, realize that is the very point where God can use us for His purpose. We must stop caring about what others might think or say, abandon unhealthy relationships, and become completely dependent on God. We must continually stay in God's word and in prayer that He will renew our minds daily and keep us focused on His will. When the enemy tried to lead Jesus away from His calling in the garden of Gethsemane, He came back at him with the word of God. We must also speak God's word against anything that hinders us from completing His work in us. So don't get mad at the people that may come against you; know that the enemy knows what great things God has in store for you and is only trying to prevent God from getting the glory in your life. But in order for God to be glorified in our lives we must not only talk the talk, but also walk the walk.

It's one thing to say we believe that God will make a way and another to act as if the way has already been made. We need to conduct our lives as if God has already done what He said He would do in our lives. For example, if you know God has called you to ministry then your behavior should reflect that of a minister. Then when God does appoint you there will be less skepticism as to whether or not you have been called because all the fruit in your life reflects that calling. In whatever we believe God will do we must walk as if it has already happened. If we believe that God is going to heal someone, then we shouldn't be planning his or her funeral. We must act as if they are healed and the same for our healing. Stop complaining and start praising! If you believe that God will give you a mate that is equally yoked and encourages your faith, why are you spending time with someone that is just the opposite? If we really believed that God would do what He said He would do we would not be worried when we lose our job, because we know that it wasn't the job that provided our needs. It was God. If God told you that He was going to give you a house, then why aren't you packing? If He said that the job was yours then why are you not studying about that position? We want God to lay everything in our lap, but that's not faith. Faith is when we walk in the dealership knowing that God will supply our need and then being willing to give the car away if God asks us to bless someone else. When we realize that it's not about the money, the car, the home, it's all about being used by God, then we can step out on faith because we have nothing to lose. We already gave it all to God.

Give liberally. We know that as Christians we should be giving, but we often put boundaries on how much we can give. Why are we so selfish with our time, our money, our gifts, and our love? For some reason we are often liberal when it comes to the things of this world and reluctant when it comes to spiritual giving. In order to receive God's best we must give Him our best. When Solomon made his request to God he first sacrificed 1000 burnt offerings. God appeared to Solomon in a dream and stated, "Ask for whatever you want me to give you" (I Kings 3:5). Solomon gave a great sacrifice and God was faithful to providing a great blessing. God was so pleased that Solomon asked for discernment to lead His people instead of displaying greed. God not only gave him wisdom, but great wealth as well. Throughout the Old Testament and New Testament God shows us that He rewards us liberally when we give liberally. Jesus tell us,

> *Give, and it will be given to you. A good measure,*
> *pressed down, shaken together and running over, will*
> *be poured into your lap. For with the measure you use,*
> *it will be measured to you. (Luke 6:38)*

We cannot give in the measure of a teaspoon and expect to receive buckets full of blessing. Whether it's our time or our resources, we must be willing to give our best. God knows your personal best and that is all He desires. However, where much is given much is required. As for our time, as a single person God requires more of me now than He ever will. When I'm married and have a family I must meet their needs as well. However, while I am single I must busy myself with my Father's business. Some of you are so worried about your future mate that you are neglecting God's calling on your life in your singleness. There are things that God wants to fulfill in us today, not tomorrow. We say one day we will do this or that for God, but let one day be today.

As for our resources, God requires that we give a tenth of all our salary, not what's left after taxes. It's good to give what is convenient, but it's better to obey what God told you to give. Sometimes God will press our hearts to give above what is required and we must realize that everything we have comes from God in the first place. Even a dog knows not to bite the hand that feeds him. When we sacrifice greatly, as Solomon, Abraham, and Joseph all did, God will give us His greatest blessing: so much that it must be pressed down, shaken together, and our life will be running over with blessings, not so we can sit back and get lazy, but so we can be a great blessing to others.

1. Have you placed limitations on what God can do in your life?

2. Can you think of ways to bless others through your giving?

Prayer

Father, I thank you for not just giving me life, but giving me life more abundantly. I pray that I walk in the abundance of your calling on my life. Lord, help me to fulfill all that you require of me. Forgive me, Father for not always seeking your divine will in my life. There are many things that may be good for me, but they are not your best. Lord in order to receive your best I must be willing to give you my best. Lord, open my eyes to see your perfect will for my life. I pray that as I seek you daily, your purpose for my life will become more and more clear. Let me not put off for tomorrow what you have called me to today. Lord, I pray that you continually strengthen me that I may stand against any distraction or hindrance to keep me from pressing forward to the high calling on my life. I pray that I step out in faith, not doubting that your word will be fulfilled. Lord, I am expecting you to do great things in my life because you are a great God. Everything that is good and perfect comes from you. Let your light be fully glorified in my life, as I give liberally of my time, my resources, and my love. Lord, I know that only what I do for you will last, so let my motives be pure. I pray on this day your kingdom come and your will be done on earth as it is in heaven. Amen.

CHAPTER 7

Driving Blind

BLIND FAITH

We tell the Lord that we are ready to receive His best in our lives and are willing to give Him our all. We take the first step and maybe even a second, but then we begin to look at our circumstances and what may appear to others as failure. At that moment our doubt starts to outweigh our faith and like Peter we begin to sink. When Peter saw Jesus walking on the water he believed that if the Lord called him he could walk on water as well. When Jesus said, "Come," Peter got out of the boat and began to walk toward Jesus (Matt. 14:29). Note that Peter waited for Jesus' command, before he took the first step. He didn't walk out in faith in himself, but in the word of his master. As Peter was walking he saw the wind trouble the waters, he began to doubt God's calling. As he was sinking he cried out for the Lord to save him. "Immediately Jesus reached out his hand and caught him. 'You of little faith," He said, "why did you doubt" (Matt. 14: 31)? Like Peter, we begin to doubt God's calling when we take our eyes off Jesus and focus on the circumstances in our environment. Regardless of what may appear as failure in your life, if you are walking in obedience to God He will never let you fail. Sometimes we also sink when we hop out of the boat with our own plan and agenda, not waiting on God's call.

I remember when I graduated from college and moved to Georgia to start graduate school. I knew that it was where God wanted me to be. I told Him that I would not go if He didn't open the door, but He did. When God calls you He always makes a way, but you still have to face the storm. Each month I could barely pay my bills and I didn't know how I was going to make it, but if I didn't stick it out my faith would have never grown. Yet, even after I completed my master's jobs were not offered. However, God was breaking my confidence in my own abilities or education. Of course we must do our best and get as much knowledge as we can, but our faith must be in God. Though Paul was extremely well educated in Judaic laws and traditions, he only wanted to take pride in the knowledge of Jesus Christ as Lord and Savior. We too may know all the scriptures by heart and know the Christian traditions, but it all is meaningless if we don't know Jesus as our Lord and Savior. Even Satan knew God's word as he twisted it to try and tempt Jesus.

When everything I did failed and I wasn't sure which road to take I had to depend on God to lead me in His word and in prayer. As we study the word we gain godly wisdom, which will truly allow us to prosper in all we do. Yet, we must continue to keep walking by faith and not by sight. We must not let doubt allow us to sink. The enemy will constantly whisper thoughts in our minds to have us believe that God has forgotten us or perhaps we misunderstood, but we must stand firm on the word of God: not just His written word, but words He has written in our hearts. God had a plan and a purpose for our lives before we were conceived in the womb. It is Satan's sole objective to destroy the plan of God in our lives. We must hold every thought captive and measure it against the word of God. If it doesn't measure up we should not acknowledge or consider the idea.

Continually remind yourself of the goal. We often get distracted when we take our eyes of the goal. Why do you think that as a basketball player goes to the line, the opposing fans behind the basket are waving streamers, yelling, and holding up signs saying "Brick"? They want the player to focus on his negative surroundings so he will begin to doubt, instead of only focusing on the goal at hand. So do whatever it takes to keep your focus. I always try to write my goals down so I can re-read and edit them as needed. Prayer is essential in order to follow God in attaining the goal. Sometimes we know what the goal is, but go about it the wrong way. God will never lead us the wrong way, which is why we must stay close to Him. Not just going to church and not just reading the Bible, but daily taking time to ask God what His will is for you on that day. We should not become so busy in trying to attain our goals that we fail to get instructions from our coach, which is God. We must stop and assess our actions and the motives for our actions. Is God pleased with how we are attaining this goal? Are we disregarding other's feelings and concerns in order to attain success? Are we complaining the entire time? Are we taking advantage of people that love and care for us? If we are, God will reveal our actions to us and we must apologize to the people we hurt as well as to God for neglecting His way.

> Create in me a pure heart, O God, and renew a steadfast spirit within me. (Ps. 51:10)

We must continually pray for God to purify our hearts. The intentions and motives of our hearts must be pure as we seek God's will for our lives. For example, if we ask God to promote us on our job or to give us a better job we must question our motives. If we want to be promoted so that we won't have to take orders, but give them, how will God teach us to follow Him if we are unwilling to follow those in authority? However, if we tell God that we want to lead others so that we might show his love, mercy, and justice to others, he can use us for his glory. David was given power, but only after he submitted to the authority of his father's household as well as to Saul. Though Saul tried to kill him, he would not strike against Saul because God anointed Saul as king. In fact David felt convicted when he cut off a piece of Saul's robe as he slept to prove he had the opportunity to kill him. David stated,

> The Lord forbid that I should do such a thing to my master, the Lord's anointed, or lift my hand against him: for he is the anointed of the Lord. (I Sam. 24:6)

God will not appoint us to positions of power if we will use that power to the detriment of His will for our lives and the lives of others. We may not actually kill them, but we could kill the will of God in their lives. We should always speak to others with the love of God and seek the Father's will above our own. When we seek him first, he has promised to provide everything we need. Though the motives of the world are driven by a lust for power, pride, and selfish ambition, our ultimate goal should be to please our Lord. To please God we often must put the needs of others before ourselves, but what we do for others will be done for us. With the same measure that we give to others it will be given unto us. David knew from personal experience that God blesses those that bless Him as he stated, "Delight yourself in the Lord and he will give you the desires of your heart" (Ps. 37:4). Once we learn to walk in step with His spirit our desires will be transformed in the image of our Father's will.

Patiently seek His will. After we have asked the Lord to purify our hearts, then we must ask that He renew a steadfast spirit within us: the spirit that He originally created before we were tainted by the cares of this world, the spirit He predestined before we were even in our mothers' womb. *Webster's* defines the word steadfast as "firmly fixed in place," "not subject to change," "firm in belief," and "faithful." Once God has called us out of the boat we must not doubt his ability to keep us from falling. When our motives are pure and we humbly seek God for guidance, we realize that we can't make it without Him and that's a good place to be, for it is the place where our faith must grow or we will sink.

God will open doors and we must have the faith to boldly walk through. God will reveal people to talk with and things we need to do and you can believe that your spirit will fight against you. Though it was my heart's desire to finish this book sometimes I just didn't feel like getting up early to pray and write. Though I would always feel better afterwards, the first steps can sometimes be a challenge. It's just like working out. We may not feel like getting up to go to the gym or get on the treadmill, but regardless of how we feel we know that it's for our benefit. Sometimes the weight of life, rejection, discouragement, and disappointment will attempt to weigh us down, but the more we resist against such pressure the stronger we will become. We must discipline ourselves to heed God's call daily, not just when we feel like it because that may never happen. Even when it may appear that our work is in vain, we must keep sowing; in due time we will reap the harvest.

God will always remain faithful to His word, but it may not be in our timing. Unfortunately, our generation is accustomed to waiting for anything. We zap our food in the microwave. We speed through the express lane. We can find out information in seconds on the Internet. We speed through life, often missing blessings because we don't want to wait. If the line is taking too long, we get out of line. If the lane we are in is moving too slow, we change lanes. People get married this week and divorced the next.

What our generation desperately needs is the type of commitment that was found in the Bible. When Jacob desired to marry Rachel he agreed to work for her Father, Laban, for seven years before he could marry her. Genesis reads, "So Jacob served seven years to get Rachel, but they seemed like only a few days to him because of his love for her" (29: 20). Some males wouldn't even consider waiting a year before they could even touch the one they loved, let alone seven years. Yet, after Jacob was tricked into marrying her older sister Leah instead of Rachel, he was willing to work another seven years for Rachel. That is the type of steadfast commitment God wants us to have towards His will for our lives. Jacob never doubted that he would receive Rachel after his work was complete, because he trusted Laban's word. How much more can we rely on the word of the Lord. Unlike man, God could never lie. The last thing we want to do is to walk away from God when we think He's taking too long. So instead of waiting for God's best we settle for temporary satisfaction. God will never give us anything before we are ready to receive it. If He does we will waste our blessing, because we are unprepared.

> *When you ask, you do not receive, because you ask with wrong motives, that you may spend what you get on your own pleasures.(Jam. 4:3)*

The book of James teaches us many lessons for seeking the will of God in our lives. It's not what we desire, but why we desire it that God questions. God would not be angry if we asked for the most extraordinary blessing, if we wanted to use it to be a blessing to others and give God glory. However, oftentimes we ask for things so that we may look with pride at our possessions, but "God opposes the proud but gives grace to the humble" (Jam. 4:6). In order to walk in faith, we must question our motives for stepping out. Even when our motives are pure, they will surely be tested by various trials. But we must understand that even the trials are part of God's will. We sometimes wrongly assume that the storms are punishment, when they are actually preparation. Before David defeated Goliath, God showed David His faithfulness in giving him the victory over a lion and a bear in his father's pasture. We ask what have we done to deserve this lion and why are we serving in this small pasture in the first place. But as David walked faithfully in the pasture, he was anointed for the palace. I know I have been tempted to leave a job or a place, but it was there that I was anointed for greater things. When we are confronted with such trials we should give God praise for His preparation.

> My brethren, count it all joy, when you fall into various trials, knowing that the testing of your faith produces patience. But let patience have its perfect work that you may be perfect and complete, lacking nothing. (Jam. 1:2-4)

Isn't it awesome to know that God wants to meet every need in our life, so much so that we are lacking no good thing? Yes, Joseph faced years of persecution, but when he was restored he lacked nothing. The more we sow, the more we will reap. So as you face rejection time and time and time again, know that God has not forgot His promise to you. God did not forget His promise to Abraham, though many doubted including his wife Sarah. Let's not let others talk us into settling for less than what God has promised. Everyone that walks by faith will be tested, before and after they are in the place God has for them. Even Jesus had to wait for His ordained time, before He could complete the work God had for Him to do. It wasn't until He was thirty that He began his ministry, yet Jesus knew of His great calling as a child. Yes Jesus knew that He was called to be more than a carpenter, but He didn't fight the process. Where you are now is not indicative of what God has for you, but we must realize that He is preparing us for greater things.

> *Let us not become weary in doing good, for at the proper time we will reap a harvest if we **do not give up**. (Gal. 6:9, NIV, emphasis mine)*

Give Him praise with each step. In order to walk by faith we must continually be thankful for what God has done, what He is doing, and what He is going to do. If we are ungrateful in the pasture we may never get to the palace. If faith is the substance of things hoped for and the evidence of things unseen (Heb. 11: 1), to walk in faith we must be confident in God's word regardless of what we see. We must fight against the temptation to complain, whine, and have our own little pity party. People will always invite us to share in their pity party, but we must stand and say "I know my God is able to do exceedingly, abundantly, above what I could even think to ask for in my life." Whether we are on the job, at school, or in church people will complain about leadership or the work given. But just as David would not strike against God's anointed, we must have respect to those in leadership and bless them regardless of how we are treated. It wasn't as if Saul was good to David: he was vindictive, jealous, and tried to kill him, but David blessed him because of the love of God in him. Maybe it's not a person, but a situation that we are tempted to complain about. I understand what it's like to not know how you're going to pay your bills or to be frustrated with your job, but we must be thankful and know that all things are working together for our good. You may be in a situation where it seems that you are the only one that stands for Christ, but is God not using you to show His light to a dying people. What is the point of shining a flashlight in a room that is well lit? If we take on their spirit of complaining and ungratefulness our light is not shining.

> Do everything without complaining or arguing so that you may become blameless and pure, children of God without fault in a crooked and depraved generation, in which you shine like stars in the universe... (Phil. 2:14 – 15, NIV)

The verse states that in order to be blameless and pure we must not murmur and bicker with one another. In order to be like Christ we must humble ourselves as Christ humbled Himself. Though He was royalty he took on the nature of a servant and was obedient to death. Even as they cried out, "Crucify Him!" Jesus asked His father's forgiveness for their sins. He did not complain, but surrendered to the will of the father. Sometimes it can be the hardest thing to hold your tongue when you know something isn't right, but we must realize that it may not be God's will for us to speak up. Maybe it's not the right time or instead of suggesting constructive solutions we are merely defending our pride and attacking the other person. God will allow others to reject us if it will bring us closer to Him. God does not want us to be dependent on people or positions. The Israelites were so dependent upon their former way of life in Egypt that they were constantly complaining to Moses and saying how it was better in Egypt. There were many times that God was so angered by their ungratefulness that He did not want them to enter the promised land. It was only because of the prayers and petitions of Moses that they were spared from receiving God's full wrath. However, they did have to spend an additional 39 years in the desert before they could make it in to Canaan. We often extend our time in the wilderness of life when we are ungrateful and too attached to our former way of life.

We must realize that regardless of what we may endure God's will is perfect. As Jesus humbled Himself to the lowest position God exalted Him to the highest position in the kingdom and "gave Him a name above every name, that at the name of Jesus every knee should bow, in heaven and on earth and under the earth" (Phil. 2: 9-10). We should never complain, knowing that we have access to our Lord through Jesus and have been made joint heirs with Christ. There is no need that God has not met. Complaining just breeds doubt and confusion, it hinders the will of God in our lives, and prevents our light from shining. We must make up our minds that regardless of the situation, the joy we have in Christ Jesus will not be taken away.

In order for us to keep the joy of Christ in our hearts we must continually have God's word in our hearts and His praise on our lips. We must daily give God praise for all His many blessings in our lives. Americans often take for granted our ability to worship our God. We are not persecuted as many of our brothers and sisters in other countries are for expressing their faith. We can thank God for all the things we never even knew He kept from harming us. It could have been someone's intent to kill us, murder us, rape us, abuse us, or rob us yesterday and God prevented it from occurring.

Even if they did rob us, we can still give Him praise just for being alive to share His goodness. Sometimes God allows things to happen so that we can be able to minister to others. We have to be thankful in good times and in bad. We cannot let our minds wander into depression, envy, or doubt. Finally,

> *Finally, brethren, whatever things are true, whatever things are noble, whatever things are just, whatever things are pure, whatever things are lovely, whatever things are of good report, if there is any virtue and if there is anything praiseworthy – meditate on these things. (Phil. 4: 8)*

1. Is there something that you are afraid to step out on faith for?

2. How can you keep your mind on the will of God?

Prayer

Lord, I pray by the power of the Holy Spirit that my faith will grow stronger with each step I take. I pray my eyes stay focused on you and my motives remain pure. I pray that I have the same commitment that Jacob had for Rachel in my pursuit of your will. The trials will quickly pass because of my great love for you and desire to please you. Let my motives be pure that you may be glorified in the end. You are not glorified when I complain or doubt your will. Forgive me Father for doubting or ungratefully questioning your will for my life. Lord, I pray that I receive every blessing in the time it was ordained for me to receive through my thankfulness. Lord, daily renew my spirit and reveal to me your purpose for each day. I thank you for the patience to remain committed to your will. I humbly give you praise for remaining committed to completing your will in me. Amen.

CHAPTER 8

Obstacle Course

THE GREAT DECEIVER

For we do not wrestle against flesh and blood, but against principalities, against powers, against rulers of the darkness of this world, against spiritual hosts of wickedness in the heavenly places. (Eph. 6:12)

When we truly seek to do the will of God it sometimes appears that our family, our friends, our spouses, and even our children have made themselves our enemies. However, we must continually remind ourselves that though they may try to deter the plan of God in our lives it is Satan that is our true enemy. He will use those closest to us to discourage us from fulfilling the will of God for our lives. This is why we discussed earlier that we must be careful of who we allow to be close to us.

Jesus understood that Satan is our adversary and the one that opposes the will of God. When the Pharisees challenged Jesus He stated that they were of their father, the devil, and that they will fulfill his lusts to murder and to lie (John 8:44).

107

Jesus stated that the devil has no truth in him, for he is the father of lies. Sometimes those that are closest to us speak lies unknowingly. Peter told Jesus that it was not the will of God that He should endure suffering and death to be resurrected again. Jesus told him, "Get behind me, Satan! You are a stumbling block to me; you do not have in mind the things of God, but the things of men" (Matt. 16:23). Peter probably believed that he had Jesus' best interest at heart according to his definition of Jesus' purpose. However, Peter's purpose was not the will of God. We must be sure of what God called us to be so that we don't allow others to mold us into their definition of what we should be. As hard as it is to accept, it is God's will for us to suffer certain things that He may be glorified.

We must rebuke Satan and not reject the people God has placed in our lives. Jesus knew that Peter would later serve Him unto death. He continued to disciple him, but He was able to recognize that the enemy was using him. We cannot always reveal to many others the plan of God in our lives. Jesus did not always want it to be known that He was the Messiah. Matthew 12:15 states, "Many followed Him, and He healed all their sick warning them not to tell who He was." It wasn't to the masses that He revealed the will of God, but to His disciples. Though they walked with Jesus daily and saw the mighty miracles that He performed it was still difficult for them to grasp who Jesus really was. Though others may not be able to comprehend what God has in store for you we already have the victory in Christ Jesus. However, we must realize that every day the enemy will try and destroy or distort the will of God in our lives.

PUT ON THE FULL ARMOR OF GOD

The moment that we accepted Jesus Christ as our Lord and Savior is the same moment we joined the army of believers. There is more to being a soldier than just believing that you are soldier. You are going into battle whether you like it or not and the key to our success is knowledge of who we are in Christ Jesus. When others accuse you wrongly and do everything in their power to defeat God's purpose in your life, "This is what the Lord says to you: 'Do not be afraid or discouraged because of this vast army. For the battle is not yours, but God's" (II Chron. 20:15). Though the battle is not ours we still must prepare ourselves in order to be used by God.

> Therefore put on the full armor of God, so that when the day of evil comes, you may be able to stand your ground, and after you have done everything, to stand. (Eph. 6: 13)

Notice how Paul continually stresses the importance of having the full armor or the whole armor of God. He could have stated that we only need to have the armor, but it is important that we recognize how each piece works in congruence with the other, just as the body has many parts and they all work together for our total health and well-being.

Belt of Truth. So we must stand with the belt of truth around our waist. The King James Version reads to be "girt about with truth" (Eph 6:14). We must encircle ourselves with truth. What truth? The truth stated in God's word and who we are in Christ Jesus. The enemy's goal is to deceive

us and cause us to doubt the word of God. When Adam and
Eve were tempted in the garden by the enemy, Eve gave the
excuse that "The serpent deceived me, and I ate" (Gen. 3:13).
The serpent convinced Adam and Eve that they would not
die, and though they did not die physically, a spiritual death
occurred. To live absent of the presence of God that they once
enjoyed was worse than physical death. Jesus stated that the
devil was a murderer from the beginning (John 8: 44). He did
not kill them physically but he convinced them to commit
spiritual suicide. Sometimes we may not completely understand why God does not want us to do something, but we
must stand on the truth that God cannot lie. If He says it will
lead to destruction it will. We use the same excuses today
that Adam and Eve used. We allow others to convince us
that what we know to be wrong is right. We also must not
allow the enemy to plant lies in our mind that only lead to
our spiritual destruction. Stop saying you cannot help but
think negatively when God has given you His divine spirit,
not of fear but of power. If we do not daily renew our minds
in the word of God we will continue to be deceived by the
enemy. We must memorize scriptures that empower us to
live boldly for Christ, such as II Timothy 1:7:

> For God has not given us the spirit of fear, but of power,
> and of love, and of a sound mind.

We must keep our minds focused on what is true. Jesus knew
that his father was true and when you know the truth the
truth will set you free (John 8: 33). Free from worry, free from
doubt, free from sin.

The Bible tells how the people perish for a lack of knowledge (Hosea 4:6). Many people are physically and spiritually dying because of their ignorance of God's word and who they are in Christ. We must be knowledgeable of what is true, so that we can keep our minds on such things and live our lives accordingly. We cannot depend solely on our pastors or other spiritual leaders to show us the truth we have to know God for ourselves. False prophets deceived the church of Thessalonica as to the day of the Lord's return, because they were not girded in true doctrine. It was even wrongly claimed that Paul and his disciples had stated this false doctrine, so he wrote them to clear up the matter and warn them not to listen to such teaching (II Thess. 2:2). Jesus warns that in the last days many will proclaim false prophesies (Matt. 24:10). Throughout history ministers have falsely prophesied the day of the Lord's return. Just three years ago people thought they would be caught up before the new millennium. But Jesus warned, "No one knows about that day or hour, not even the angels in heaven, not the Son, but only the Father" (Matt. 24:36). All this is to say that we must know what the Word of God says for ourselves, not just what others say the Word of God says. There are things that God may require of you that He will only reveal to you, which is why we must know the truth for ourselves.

Breastplate of Righteousness. We must also guard our heart with the breastplate of righteousness (Eph: 6: 14). Once we know the truth we have the power to walk in righteousness. We must first understand what is meant by the word righteousness. According to *Strong's Exhaustive Concordance* the Greek word for righteousness as used in this context is *dikaiosune,* meaning equity of character or act and also implying justification. Other derivatives also imply "to be made right", or "to be cleansed." When we accepted Christ we were given the free gift of righteousness and justification. We are justified by our faith in Christ, which should result in just actions. To live righteously does not mean to live a perfect life, but to strive to be upright in all our ways. The Bible states how Abraham's faithfulness was counted to him as righteousness (Gen. 15:16). James reveals that he was justified by his obedience to offer his son as a sacrifice (2:21). James also states how Rahab, the prostitute, was also justified or made righteous by her obedience. Though these were not perfect people their obedient faith justified them before God. The enemy is a deceiver and may try to convince you that it is not possible for you to be considered as righteous or justified in God's eyes, but that is a lie. Christ died that we might have the power to walk in His divine nature, justified by our faith. Our faith should radically effect how we live. How do we know if we are living a righteous life? Well the Bible gives several illustrations of how the righteous live.

As we have seen in the examples of Abraham and Rahab, the righteous are obedient to the word of the Lord. Abraham was willing to sacrifice the son that he had waited for a quarter of a century to have. Rahab put her life and the lives of her family in danger by giving shelter to the messengers of God. We are not walking in the breastplate of righteousness if we are only obedient to what is convenient for us. The righteous, give generously to others and also show mercy (Ps. 37: 21). When you are continually generous to others God will not only bless you, but your family and future generations as

He did with the families of both Abraham and Rahab. David stated,

> *I was young and now I am old yet I have never seen the righteous forsaken or their children begging for bread. (Ps. 37: 25, NIV)*

Many of us are not even blessed for our own righteousness, but because of the righteousness of our parents and grandparents. When I was little and sang the song "Father Abraham," I had no idea of the magnitude of what I was singing when I proclaimed to be a child of Abraham. Even if your parents or grandparents did not walk with God, your spiritual heritage makes you a child of God. Because of your faithfulness your children and grandchildren will be blessed for your righteousness.

The word also tells us that the righteous speak words of wisdom and judgment (Ps. 37:30). James tells us that true wisdom does not come from the world but from God. The wisdom of this world promotes selfish ambition and envy.

> *But the wisdom that comes from above is first pure; then peaceable, considerate, submissive, full of mercy and good fruit, impartial and sincere. (James 3:17)*

Gospel of Peace. Paul's instructed us to also have "your feet fitted with readiness that comes from the gospel of peace" (Eph. 6: 15). We should be perpetually ready to share the gospel or good news of peace with others. Though we are soldiers for Christ our goal is to establish peace, not to breed strife. Some people seem to enjoy instigating arguments, strife, and discontentment. We should not seek to justify ourselves to others, but to allow God to use us to bring peace. Remember that the battle is not ours: it's the Lord's. When Jesus was accused He did not try to justify Himself and He did not argue. Jesus knew that God would justify Him in just three days. When you are confident in God's plan and purpose you do not take accusatory remarks of others to heart.

Timothy warns us to "Flee the evil desires of youth, and pursue righteousness, faith, love and peace" (II Tim. 2: 22). It will not always be easy to walk in peace with others and we must pursue it diligently. Many great men and women were and are persecuted when they have stood for peace. We honor the lives of Dr. Martin Luther King Jr., Coretta Scott King, and former president Jimmy Carter for their vigilant pursuit of peace, yet the very people they desired to help also persecuted them. When you are not intimidated or angered when others are enraged they often become even more enraged that you are not sinking to their level. To seek peace does not mean that you don't take a stand, for it is the strongest stance you can make. When you do speak it will not be out of anger or pride, but from a heart of righteousness.

If you must always have the last word then you are not pursuing peace and righteousness. As a child I would always be reprimanded for trying to get the last word in, but as I grew in Christ that became less and less important. Not to say that it isn't tempting at times when in actuality we are correct but, it's more important that we glorify God not ourselves. When my mom was teaching me to drive, whether or not I had the right of way was not always the most important thing. Sometimes you have to let people go ahead, instead of being dead right. Timothy states that we should have nothing to do with "foolish and stupid arguments, because you know they only produce quarrels" (II Tim. 2:23). So what can we do? We pray and the word states that, "The prayer of a righteous man is powerful and effective" (I Peter 5: 16). The word also tells us that the Lord's eyes are on the righteous and He is attentive to our cries and will deliver them from **all** their troubles (Ps. 34: 15-17). Though the wicked may cry out the Lord is not attentive to their cry as He is to the righteous. When we revere the Lord and truly try to live in obedience to His will we gain special access to our Father's heart.

Shield of Faith. The King James version of this verse states "above all" other pieces of armor we must have faith. I believe this to be true in light of Hebrew 11, which counts all the people in the Bible that were considered righteous for their faith: Abel, Enoch, Noah, Abraham, Joseph, Moses, Rahab, etc. The breastplate of righteousness and the shield of faith go hand and hand. You cannot walk in God's righteousness without faith in God. Noah was considered righteous because of his faith. "By his faith he condemned the world and became heir of the righteousness that comes by faith" (Heb. 11:7). It was because of Abraham's unwavering faith that he was considered as righteous.

> He did not waver at the promise of God through unbelief, but was strengthened in faith, giving glory to God, and being fully convinced that what He had promised He was able to perform. And therefore "it was accounted to him for righteousness." (Rom. 4: 20-22)

We will not lead victorious lives if we do not believe and trust in the God of our salvation. How can we stand boldly against wickedness if we do not believe God stands with us? We must know that if God be for us, it doesn't matter who may be against us. Jesus could not believe that His disciples were of such little faith that they feared the storm when their Savior was right there with them. We must believe as David did, that God has already given us the victory over every giant in our life. David proclaims,

> The Lord is my light and my salvation; whom shall I fear? The Lord is the strength of my life – of whom shall I be afraid? (Ps. 27: 1)

There are things that God has given us the victory in that we do not possess because of our lack of faith. Once we believe that God is so much bigger than any obstacle then we will be able to claim the victory that God has been ready and waiting to release in your life. It is impossible for us to please God without faith. In order to walk in the full armor of God, we must be faithful and obedient to God's word, not wavering back and forth and doubting whether God will come through. We cannot expect to receive anything from the Lord if we are double-minded and unstable in our faith (Jam. 1:7-8). Through our faith God is able to provide his salvation in our time of trouble. By faith we are saved.

Helmet of Salvation. The salvation of God covers our head that we might have the mind of God and be protected from the plan of the wicked one. Salvation begins when we repent of our sins and confess Jesus Christ as our Lord and Savior. Not only has God given us eternal life and saved us from going to hell, He can save us from living in hell on earth.

Before Jesus manifested on earth the Israelites relied on God to protect them from their enemies and save them from the trials of the world. Many times when people refer to God's salvation they are speaking of God's deliverance and defense of His people. In Exodus as the Israelites leave Egypt with Pharoah's army hot on their trail, Moses declares,

> *Do not be afraid. Stand still, and see the salvation of the Lord, which He will accomplish for you today. (Ex. 14: 13)*

It is obvious that Moses was protected by the full armor of God. Pharoah's army is right on their trail seeking to kill them and yet he tells them to be still. It's clear that he is speaking in faith, when we know that Moses' natural man wanted to run, as our flesh would as well. When he killed the Egyptian, what did he do? He ran to the wilderness. However, in the wilderness God revealed himself so miraculously that he knew he would never have to run in fear again. So he tells the Israelites to be still and wait for the salvation of the Lord for they will never have to fear the Egyptians again. Yet also he tells them to hold their peace as they wait. As a general in the Lord's army, Moses was able to look at the Egyptians fiercely pursuing behind them and the Red Sea in front of them and not waver to the left or to the right. When you boldly stand for God he is obligated to boldly and miraculously defend you. The Lord immediately responds to Moses' cry for help and tells the Israelites to move forward and Moses to raise his staff and stretch his hands forth to part the water (Ex. 14: 18). The Angel of the Lord and the cloud of God, which were leading the Israelites, moved behind them so that the armies of Pharaoh could not reach the Israelites. The cloud gave the light of day to one side and continuous darkness of night to the other. When we let go and let God have the victory, He does things in such a miraculous way that there is no way man could be glorified, only God.

As amazing as the story of Israel's deliverance was, some of you still doubt God's power today. The same God that will save then can save now. The only hindrance is our lack of extraordinary faith. Here is a modern day account of God's miraculous salvation in our time. My mother once knew a woman that was abused by her father since childhood. As she grew older she moved from place to place to avoid her father's wrath. The more she ran the more enraged he became. He often told her that one day he would find her and kill her. One day her Father found her and as she was walking she saw him coming toward her with a gun in hand. She decided that she couldn't run any longer and she paused and said a silent prayer for God's deliverance. Her father was quickly approaching with his hand on the trigger when suddenly he fell to the ground. He had a heart attack and died on the spot.

If you still don't believe that God can deliver you from any situation today as He did in biblical times then you should re-evaluate what type of salvation you possess. If we believe that God is all-powerful, all knowing, and everywhere all at the same time, then why can we not call on Him in our times of distress? The key to having victory in Christ is knowing the great power that we have access to and then having the faith to do what He tells you to do, regardless of how illogical it may appear to others. When God told Joshua to march around the walls of the city of Jericho, it may not have appeared logical to some, but when the walls came crashing down they had to give God all the glory and praise. When God fights your battles, the world will stand back in amazement and give glory to God.

Sword of the Spirit. We must stand with the helmet of salvation and defend ourselves with the sword of the spirit, which is the all-powerful word of the living God. The Greek translation for word is *rhema*, the "all-powerful word or command of God." Though this applies to the written word of God it is not limited to only the written word of God. When Jesus pulls out His sword of the spirit against Satan He states, "It is written man does not live on bread alone, but on every word that comes from the mouth of God" (Matt. 4:4). Though Satan could quote the word of God he did not use it in the spirit it was given. To stand on God's word and use it effectively, we must first walk in faith and obedience to that word. Jesus was quoting Deuteronomy 8: 3, which reads,

> *He humbled you, causing you to hunger and then feeding you with manna, which neither you nor your fathers had known, to teach you that man does not live on bread alone but on every word that comes from the mouth of the Lord.*

When the Israelites were in the wilderness for forty years, God continued to provide for their every need. He maintained them so well that their clothes did not even wither. When the enemy comes against us and takes every worldly possession we must stand on God's word that He is

Jehovah-Jireh, our provider. He didn't provide in a way that was familiar to them or their fathers. God will exceed our expectations when we trust Him to provide. When God speaks heaven and earth stand at attention. Job learned the goodness of God in His tribulation and the power of His word. God revealed how powerful the word of the Lord is to Job, when He proclaimed,

> *Have you commanded the morning since your days began, And caused the dawn to know its place. (Job 38:12)*

Everything must surrender to the awesome power of God's word. Why should we fear when the enemy may stand encamped around us, if we have the power of the living God in our possession when we call on His name and speak His word in faith? Moses parted the Red Sea at the Lord's command. Joshua crossed over the Jordan. What Jordan exists in your life that you must speak the word of God to overcome?

Every day we must pray that God empower us to walk in the full armor of God. We are naked prey to the enemy without it. Every piece of armor works together: the sword of the spirit, the breastplate of righteousness, the gospel of peace, the belt of truth, and above all the shield of faith. We are protected and given the sword to attack the enemy with. We should not just allow the enemy to use us as a punching bag when we have the armor to defend ourselves with. Oftentimes this defense will confuse the enemy as well as the world. Jesus always was covered by the full armor and yet sometimes appeared defenseless in the eyes of man because of His peaceful demeanor. Yet at other times Jesus attacked the hypocrisy of man, when others saw it as no big deal. We should never respond to conflict in a way that is expected by man, but in a way that glorifies God. To do this we must always walk in the full armor of God.

1. Are there particular pieces of armor that you forget to put on?

2. Are there any areas in which you question God's will or whether not you truly have victory?

Prayer

Lord I give you all the praise and glory for having given me the victory in every spiritual battle. Lord I pray that I realize when the enemy is using people in my life to come against your will. Let me reject the enemy and yet still love your people. Lord renew my mind in your truth daily. Continue to reveal yourself to me, as well as who I am in you. Each day let me take on the whole armor of God, so that I do not fall into the traps of the enemy. Lord, let me surround myself in truth. Lord I pray that I wear the breastplate of righteousness, in all I do let me be holy as you are holy. Thank you for your justification and for cleansing me of all unrighteousness. Now that I have the victory over sin let me live a victorious life. Let me always pursue the peace you have given me in Christ Jesus. Above all, let me never lose faith in your promises to me. Help me to know and use your sword more effectively against my enemy. When my enemy surrounds me let me realize that you are only a prayer away. Let me pray in the power of your Holy Spirit in every situation. I thank you that the battle is not mine for you are my mighty fortress and my salvation. Praise to your name forever and ever. Amen.

CHAPTER 9

Seize the Vision

I will pour out my Spirit on all people. Your sons and daughters will prophesy, your young men will see visions, your old men will dream dreams. (Acts 2:17)

What visions has God given you? Not who the world says you are or perhaps even who your parents say you are: what we desperately need to know is who does God says we are. We may have our own desires and plans but they will never fulfill us in the way that His calling will. Regardless of what others may think we have to stand on who God says that we are. Some of you may not realize that the vision you had was actually from God. You know that it was God because it is bigger than anything you could have thought of on your own and you don't even fully understand the revelation. What God has called you to do will allow Him to be glorified in your life. If what you desire to do only gives you glory and makes you appear important in man's eyes then this was not from God. But what God has called you to will always give Him glory. Whether you are a minister or a doctor you will be aiding the body of Christ. Whether you are a lawyer or a prophet you can call out for God's righteousness and justice for His people. Whether you are a stay-at-home mother or a teacher you will be shaping and molding young minds in the knowledge of Jesus Christ. Whatever you do will bless your life, as well as the lives of others. There are things that God has called only you to do. No other person can perform that task in the way that you can. You were specifically designed with this purpose in God's mind.

The closer you draw to God the closer He will draw to you (Jam. 4:8). As the Father pours His spirit upon you, you will begin to see His vision for your life as well as for others. Joseph did not only dream of his future as a leader, but also the death of the cupbearer. God gives dreams not only of success, but also of destruction. He allows us to see both good and bad so that we will be prepared when the vision comes to pass and so we are not devastated in the end.

I had applied for a job that I truly believed I would receive. I had experience and abilities that would be compatible for the position. One night I dreamed that I would not receive the position. I knew the dream was from God yet I was upset and didn't want to accept it. However, in time I could see how God opened other doors and that position would have taken away from the work I would do to glorify him, for example the writing of this book. So when I received word that I didn't get the position I was not devastated by the report. We must understand that the world is not our provider: God is, and He will meet every need with or without a job. When there was no food in the wilderness God met their need and released manna from the sky. Peter left his profitable business as a fisherman to follow Christ and from that point on the Lord supplied every thing he needed. We may not understand or be excited by the vision at first. I'm sure that there was a point in time when Jesus saw the vision of his purpose on earth and was not overjoyed by the news. In fact, Jesus prayed that if it were His Father's will to allow the cup to pass from Him. However, Jesus stated, "not my will, but yours be done" (Lk.22: 42). The Bible tells us that Jesus prayed so earnestly that He began to sweat drops of blood (Lk.22: 44). He was about to lose His life and the disciples that pledged their lives to Him could not even stay up to pray with Him. People may say they love you and will support you to the end, but we must know that our help comes from the Lord. Though the disciples could not stay awake, God sent an angel to Jesus to strengthen Him in His time of need (Lk. 22:43). Though Christ suffered the greatest tribulation, it allowed us to receive salvation and gave him ultimate power over life and death.

Sometimes we must suffer in order to be a blessing to others, but God always blesses us in return. However, don't serve in order to be blessed: serve because it is the right thing to do. In all that we do and say we should show the love of God. The mission God has planned for you will not always be easy, but His strength is made perfect in our weakest moment.

So What's Your Mission?

Christ fulfilled the mission that His Father gave to Him and we too must take up our cross and fulfill the mission that our Father has for our lives. What would you do not for money, but simply because of your passion? We are all given gifts and abilities by God to complete the mission He has for our lives. We might not completely understand the complexities of the journey we are on and that's okay. All we need to do is have faith that God will fulfill His work in us. Some of you know what it is you are called to do and are hindered by your desire to know all the details. Well if you knew all the details it wouldn't require faith. God will reveal what you need to know as you continually step out on faith. Be careful not to question God in doubt. Obviously, God knows that whatever He speaks will come to pass, so to question His ability to perform His word is an assault on His character. When the angel of the Lord told Zechariah that his wife would bear a son he questioned, "How can I be sure of this? I am an old man and my wife is well along in years" (Luke 1: 18). From that point on Zechariah was not able to speak until after John's birth. Now the Bible tells us that Zechariah was an upright man who served in the priesthood, yet he still was able to doubt the word of the Lord from the mouth of an angel. Though it is important to serve God, you cannot please God without faith. We have said to the Lord "I am too young, too old, too broke, too unqualified," and God is disheartened by our lack of faith. Even if we don't understand how the vision will come to pass, we cannot doubt that it will come to pass.

FREEDOM IN CHRIST

It is for freedom that Christ has set us free. Stand firm then, and do not let yourselves be burdened by a yoke of slavery. (Gal. 5:1)

Sometimes in trying to attain God's will in our lives we can lose sight of the big picture. Though He was criticized, Christ took time to give healing even on the Sabbath. His love for God liberated Him from tradition and ritual. Christ came that we might live life more abundantly. Many of us are not living life abundantly because we are still enslaved to the laws of man and conform to the image of this world. The world system should not have any influence on what we do or don't do. For example, if God tells you to start a business that will give God glory, that would go against the law of man to have stability in working for someone else. However, if that is what God has called you to do then know that He has already given you everything you need. When I talk with college students about what they want to do many of them base their decisions on which career will allow them to make the most money, what major is acceptable to their parents, or on what the world categorizes as a successful career. Their decisions are not based on what will truly satisfy them and utilize the God-given talents they possess. Before you decide on a definite career path, spend some time in that industry as an intern or volunteer. Since I was a little girl I always said I'd be a teacher or a lawyer, because I always enjoyed helping people. I think I chose to study law because I thought it would be more profitable. In college I had the opportunity to do a summer internship with the Department of Justice. It was truly a great experience, but in the end I came to the conclusion that though I am passionate about justice, I didn't want to go into law. I had this Hollywood view of the excitement and drama of being a lawyer, when in actuality it can be just as monotonous as any other profession. So there

I was entering my junior year majoring in political science and realizing I didn't want to go to law school. Because I had taken additional courses I could have graduated early, but I chose to double major in speech communication, not realizing that God was preparing me to be the speech professor and speaker I am today. Even when we don't know where we are going, God will order our footsteps and plant us in the places where He desires us to be, but we must seek His will in our lives. With every decision I prayed, "Lord if this is your will, you have to open a door and if it's not your will close the door." When He opens the door and tells us to go we must not hesitate.

If you know that God has called you to something else, you must go. Like Abraham, you may not understand fully where God is calling you to but that's where faith steps in. Everything we need our Father has already provided. If we are children of the king, we walk in His authority and blessing wherever we are. My college roommate, always knew she wanted to work in the Christian music industry and did internships all throughout college with different record companies. After graduation she knew that she would have to move to Tennessee without a job, to pursue this goal, but with a whole lot of faith she packed up and moved. She landed a job with a growing Christian record company and is fulfilling the purpose that God has for her life. She had prepared for the open door God placed before her and boldly walked through. God will always prepare you for what He has called you to, even if you don't realize what you are being prepared for. Looking back I had no idea what God was doing, but now I understand in part why He did what

He did in my life. We must not be afraid to go into industries and professions and challenge the traditional world systems. In Romans we are told, "Do not conform any longer to the image of this world, but be transformed by the renewing of your mind"(12:2). Wherever we are we should influence the culture and systems in our environment to reflect that of the kingdom of God and not of this world. Don't be surprised if God asks you to do something that has never been done before. God created the world from nothing; surely He must be able to use us to bring about new ideas, new inventions, new cures, and a new way of thinking. We must continually allow God to renew our mind in Him and remove the traditions and expectations of this world.

> Beware lest anyone cheat you through philosophy and empty deceit, according to the tradition of men, according to the basic principles of this world and not according to Christ. (Col. 2:8)

We cannot enter into a new level in the things of God by following man-made traditions. We need to question whether we are doing something for worldly status or because it's the will of God. There are times when you knew you shouldn't have done something; though it may have appeared right in man's eyes, in your heart you knew it wasn't what you were called to do. What's good is not the same as what's best. Saul disobeyed God in order to gain the acceptance of man and lost his reign as king for his disobedience. Do not let anyone hold you captive to human traditions and customs when Jesus Christ has liberated you. Some of you are still fighting the fact that you have allowed others to enslave you and keep you from fulfilling your true potential. Anyone that truly loves you will want you to have the best even if it is not their will. I'm sure that Mary did not want to see Jesus crucified, but she had to submit to the will of God. No parent wants to see their child suffer, but they must release their child to God realizing that God truly wants what's best for His children.

Are you your worst enemy? We have discussed the importance of not allowing people or circumstances to keep you from attaining your rightful place in God. However, it may not be others that are keeping you bound. It could be you. God will not force us to walk with Him. He has given us free will to choose how we want to live. Some of you are choosing to live below what God has called for your life. When we willfully disobey God and do things contrary to His will we are choosing death. Our dreams will die, our finances will dry up, our marriages will crumble, and even bring about illness and physical death. If you believe just enough to make it into heaven, the agony and pain of seeing what miraculous things God wanted to do in your life that you didn't believe he could do would be torture. God tells us that,

> I call heaven and earth as witnesses today against you, that I have set before you life and death, blessings and curses; therefore choose life, that both you and your descendants may live. (Deut. 30: 19)

Regardless of how bleak your situation may appear on the surface that is the very point where God can do a miraculous work so great that people will look at you in disbelief and say "God has done an awesome work in your life!" Some of you have come to the point where you feel that death would be easier than living through the pain. I say yes you should choose death: not physically but to all the former things that have bound you in chains. Death to depression, death to unforgiveness, death to sin, death to fear, death to anxiety, death to every stronghold that exalts itself against the will of God and life to the spirit of God in you, life to you and all the generations that proceed you.

> *I will not die, but live, and declare the works of the Lord. (Ps. 118:17)*

Don't wrongfully assume that your life does not affect the lives of others. God wants to use us to be a blessing to others. The very trial that we have gone through or are going through, God will use to help someone else to pass his or her test. It is selfish and self-centered of us to waste our lives on meaningless pursuits when God wants to use us for His good pleasure. When we hold fast to God and allow Him to be our life, not only is our life blessed but also the lives of our family, friends, and children. You may say it's too hard but God says "Now what I am commanding you is not too difficult for you or beyond your reach"(Deut. 30:11). You must convince yourself that it is God in you that will allow you to succeed. When we obey God completely and trust in Him totally He will withhold no good thing from us. His word says that we will be blessed wherever we go, our children will be blessed, and when we come in we will be blessed, as well as when we go out. Those that come against us will be defeated. Every work we set out to do the Lord will bless and give us prosperity.

The Lord will open to you His good treasure, the heavens, to give rain on your land in its season, and to bless all the work of your hand. You shall lend to many nations but shall not borrow. And the Lord shall make you the head and not the tail; you shall be above only and not beneath, if you heed the commandments of the Lord your God, which I command you today, and are careful to observe them. (Deut.28:12-13)

However, the very opposite will occur when we go against the will of God. Not only are we cursed, but also our family and future generations will be devastated. Our storehouses will dry up and the work of our hands will be fruitless. God gives us choice, but this should be the easiest decision you ever make. There is no sin, relationship, fortune or fame worth losing the blessing of God over your life. With God in your life nothing is impossible.

NOTHING IS TOO HARD FOR GOD!

You may be saying that you do not have adequate resources or abilities to fulfill the work God has given you to do, but nothing is too hard for God. Whatever the situation, whatever the circumstance, God has already made a way for you to come out on top. Did He not promise us that if we follow His commands we would be on top and not below? When Sarah doubted that she would truly bear a child in her old age the Lord said to Abraham, "Why did Sarah laugh and say, 'Will I really have a child, now that I am old?' Is anything to hard for the Lord? I will return to you at the appointed time next year and Sarah will have a son" (Gen. 18: 13-14). Sarah tried to deny that she laughed, but you can't hide anything from God. God hears us when we say "This will never happen." We may be able to fool others but God knows our hearts. We must be convinced beyond a shadow of a doubt that God is more than able to fulfill His work in us. However, it must be fulfilled in its appointed time. For Sarah that time would be the following year. Perhaps Sarah would have given birth earlier if she had believed God sooner. We don't always know why things are delayed, but when we persistently trust God He blesses us even in the midst of trials.

Don't look at trials and rejection as an indication of your failure, but as proof of your success. Through trials and through rejection you become stronger and God is able to perfect His work in you. Was not Jesus rejected even by prestigious religious leaders of His day for challenging their hypocritical faith? When He spoke with the authority as the Son of God the high priest accused Jesus of blasphemy! "Then they spat in His face and struck Him with their fists. and some slapped Him in His Face, 'Prophesy to us, You Christ (the Messiah)! Who was it that struck you?'"(Matt.26:67-68, AMP) People may laugh and mock you, but in the end God will not be mocked. God will be glorified in you if you remain faithful despite rejection.

Though Jesus was rejected by men He reigned at the right hand of God. Yes, we may be denied but God said we would be the head and not the tail. We will not give people credit or attribute our success to our own ability. We will say "the Lord has done this and it is marvelous in our eyes" (Ps. 118: 23). Though it may be the same day we are rejected we should rejoice and know that this too is the day the Lord has made and we will rejoice because we know that there is nothing impossible for our Father. Jesus did not argue and fight because He knew His Father only allowed Him to suffer so that He could reign as King of Kings. When you keep your focus on the final outcome you are able to look past the pain.

1. What talents, gifts, or understanding does God want you to use for His glory?

2. What can you begin doing today to pursue the mission God has given you?

Prayer

Heavenly Father I praise your great and awesome name. For you alone are God Almighty and you alone reign on high. Thank you for allowing me to be called a child of the king. While I was yet in sin you called me to yourself and gave my life purpose and meaning. You have set before me the choice of life or death and I will choose life. Lord, help me to walk in your perfect will and remove all the things that seek to destroy your vision for my life. My only fear will be what would happen if I don't obey your word. I will not fear what people may say or do. I thank you for helping me to hold every thought captive and not allowing my mind to conform to the thoughts of this world. Renew my mind as I meditate on your word. There is no obstacle that I cannot overcome in you, for I can do all things through Christ that strengthens me. You have made me the head and not the tail. Every word that you have spoken over my life must come to pass. Lord I pray I do not just live, but that I live in your abundance. To you I will give all the praise, glory, and honor for all the wonderful things you have done. Amen.

CHAPTER 10

Staying in Your Lane

For the revelation waits an appointed time; it speaks of
the end and will not prove false. Though it linger, wait
for it will certainly come and will not delay.

(*Habakkuk 2:3*)

We cannot allow time and unexpected circumstances to
cause us to doubt what we know God has called us to do.
You realize that the mission itself is bigger than you, but the
battle is not yours; it's the Lord's. Each day you walk in the
whole armor of God and each day you expect to reach the
place where God told you to go. You continue to look for the
promise. Yet, you see no evidence of it's coming. You begin
to feel discouraged by circumstances that are contrary to
the vision. The prophet Habakkuk is disgusted by the injus-
tice of his time. He states, "Therefore the law is powerless,
and justice never goes forth. For the wicked surround the
righteous; therefore perverse judgment proceeds"(Hab. 1:4).
Habakkuk cries to the Lord for justice for the righteous. He
says to himself that he will wait for the Lord's reply to his
plea for help. The Lord first tells Habakkuk to write down

the vision God had given him and to make it easily understandable for all. God often gives us visions that are complex in our minds, but we must take the time to analyze and interpret the vision. Then God tells Habakkuk that He has not forgotten him but the revelation must wait for its appointed time. Though it may linger it will definitely come and you will see the manifestation of the vision.

Many times we do not realize that the vision God has given us has a particular time and season in which it will take place. Now some of us are in the season but have not cultivated the seed God has placed in our heart. Many times we do not even realize how God is pruning us and shaping us for the work He has for our lives. Yet when we look back we can see how God had prepared us. Though the pruning process is painful, we must endure it in order to be able to produce a great harvest for God.

Every branch in Me that does not bear fruit He takes away; and every branch that bears fruit He prunes, that it may bear more fruit. (John 15:1-3)

Sometimes we feel as if we have been pruned: cut off from family, friends, and familiar comforts. We must understand that the emptiness is not loneliness because God has never left our side. As empty vessels we can be filled with God's glory. He has brought us to a place where we must rely on Him and Him alone. God may cut us off from relationships that are not bearing fruit in our lives. We also must make the decision to not return to those unfruitful relationships. Stop trying to reconnect with what God has cut off. We may feel abandoned, not realizing that God only prunes those He loves and wants to prosper even more. The Greek word *kathairo*, interpreted as "prune" above, also means "to cleanse" or "to purify" according to *Strong's Exhaustive Concordance*. The same word is also used in Hebrew 10:2, to explain how the blood of Christ has cleansed us once-and-for-all. Yet just as Christ was continually purged and purified so are we. God's glory will never be fully revealed in us when we are consumed by our own desires.

DYING TO SELF

And as for us, why do we endanger ourselves every hour? I die every day – I mean that, brothers – just as surely as I glory over you in Christ Jesus our Lord. (I Cor. 15: 30-31, NIV)

When Paul was given the revelation of Christ on the road to Damascus, everything he stood on was shaken. In order to become the man of God he was called to be he had to continually die to himself. As a follower of Christ Jesus he was reborn and made new. So now Paul explains to fellow believers that the glory of God is endangered when we do not daily die to ourselves. Every day we must make a conscious decision to live for Christ. We have so much to gain when we walk in Him that it's foolish to endanger what we have in Christ to be joined to this world. We must allow God to prune us of unhealthy habits, addictions, dependencies, and behaviors. Where we are going God is not going to allow our former self to come along. Paul made it clear that though he stood in God's glory, it is only because he daily died to himself. We too must die to our former selves in order to attain the glory God has already predestined for our lives. In the same chapter he tells the church of Corinth not to be fooled into thinking that they will be able to carry former behaviors as well as negative associations through the door that God has opened for your life.

> Do not be misled: "Bad company corrupts good charac-
> ter." Come back to your senses as you ought, and stop
> sinning; for there are some who are ignorant of God – I
> say this to your shame. (I Cor. 15: 33)

It is said that one bad apple spoils the whole bunch. It is time for us to pay attention to the rotten apples that God is revealing in our lives. Not just acknowledge that they are rotten, but then to remove them from our lives. Some things you are not just going to walk away from easily. Some things will require prayer as well as fasting. If even Jesus had to fast forty days and forty nights and be tempted by the enemy, what makes us think that we can just walk right into the blessings of God without preparation? The disciples learned this lesson as they tried to command a demon out of a little boy. The Father brought the child to Jesus after the disciples could not cast out the unclean spirit and asked Jesus if he could heal his son. Jesus questioned whether the father believed and reminded him that all things are possible when you believe. The father responded, "I do believe; help me overcome my unbelief" (Mk.9:24). Jesus then rebuked the evil spirit and he left the boy. The disciples later questioned God as to why they could not rebuke the evil spirit and Jesus stated,

*This kind can come out by nothing but by prayer and
fasting. (Mk. 9:29)*

How does this story relate to dying to self? Well, some spir-
its of flesh may have immediately been defeated when you
decided to walk with Christ. However, there are some things
in your life that leave you wondering why they are not as
easily shaken. These will only be defeated by prayer and
fasting, if you have truly decided to walk away from them.
You can pray and fast and though you have been released
from their bondage, you choose to be bound by that sin once
more. In both the Old and New Testament people have given
themselves to prayer and fasting in repentance of sin. In the
book of Nehemiah the Israelites not only fasted and prayed
for their own sins but the sins of their forefathers, stating,
"But they our forefathers, became arrogant and stiff-necked,
and did not obey your commands. They refused to listen
and failed to remember the miracles you performed among
them" (Neh. 9:16-17). In order to walk in God's will on this
journey we must pray that we be released from our sins as
well as the sins of former generations, generational afflictions of alcoholism, diseases, abuse, sins of lust and pride,
poverty, depression, and the list goes on. Praise be to God
that whatever we ask for in His name will be given to us! It is
not the Father's will for us to live in any of these afflictions.
So we have the right to ask for His deliverance not only for
us but for others as well. Daniel also prayed and fasted that
the people of Israel be given God's mercy for their sins and
delivered from the wrath of God (Dan. 9). David prayed and
fasted for deliverance from persecution and for God's judg-

ment of his persecutors. Time after time David was delivered from his enemies, as he was from Saul. Saul was judged accordingly. David was known as a man after God's own heart (I Sam. 13:14). David was not perfect but he continually sought the presence of God in his life through worship and prayer. David wrote numerous psalms and prayers for deliverance, praise, and purification. We too must hunger for God in both good times and bad. David prayed and fasted for the healing of his son and for others (II Sam. 12:16; Ps. 35:13). We too must fast and pray for the healing of others as well as for our own healing. It may be a fast from secular movies, TV, music, or anything else that is feeding your flesh and not your spirit.

Sometimes it is not physical healing we need, but emotional healing from past hurts and wounds. We must forgive as Christ has forgiven us and many times that involves praying for emotional healing and restoration. We cannot love others with the love of Christ when we continually hold past hurts and unforgiveness against others. Our relationships with others are so much better when we have let go of old baggage. Remember that we must pack light on this journey. For all we will ever need, we have in Christ Jesus.

Since we have these promises, dear friends, let us purify ourselves from everything that contaminates body and spirit, perfecting holiness out of reverence for God. (II Cor. 7:1, NIV)

DON'T LOOK BACK

Jeremiah has been known as the "reluctant prophet" as he hesitated to take on the roll as a prophet (Jer.1:6). However, once he accepted the call he never looked back. His ministry and life exemplify what it means to die to self and of undying faith. Jeremiah continued to walk in faith, dying to flesh, because of his reverence and fear of the Lord. Throughout his ministry he was persecuted, ignored, criticized, tortured, and ridiculed, yet he could not abandon his call from God. The people of Israel continued to turn their back on God and worship false idols. They had strayed away from the devotion of their youth and became as ungrateful as their forefathers. They were originally of the few that were allowed into the Promised Land by Joshua. Though many of their parents did not cross over with them they carried with them the generational curse of idolatry and unfaithfulness to God. Jeremiah proclaimed this word of the Lord to Jerusalem,

> *I remember the devotion of your youth, how as a bride*
> *you loved me and followed me through the desert,*
> *through a land not shown. Israel was holy to the Lord"*
> *(Jer. 2:2-3, NIV)*

In their youth they were obedient to God and He brought them to a land of abundance and prosperity, unlike their forefathers who were afraid to possess the land God had given them. However, this generation became too comfortable in the blessings of God. They began to lose their reverence or fear of God. Though they knew how God punished their forefathers for their idolatry and continually looking back to the former days in Egypt, they assumed that they could worship other gods and not be judged. Though their ancestors were enslaved in Egypt they had so little faith they thought that it would be better for them there. Just as their ancestors had done, the younger generation would leave the Promised Land to go back to Egypt. Jeremiah proclaims,

> *And now why take the road to Egypt, to drink the waters of Sihor? Or why take the road to Assyria, to drink the waters of the River? Your own wickedness will correct you, and your backsliding will rebuke you. Know therefore and see that it is an evil and bitter thing that you have forsake the Lord your God, and the fear of Me is not in you. (Jer. 2:18- 19)*

It's easy to look at the Israelites and say how ungrateful they were to God and yet not see the similarities in our own generation. At least they were faithful to God in their youth. Society excuses the immorality of youth and young adults, by accounting their sinful nature as being directly associated with their age. Regardless of age, once you acknowledge and accept Christ as your Lord and Savior you have the power to live a righteous life. Look at Jeremiah, look at Esther, and look at David: though they were young in age they showed tremendous faith and obedience to God. How can we strive to live righteously in our own lives? Revere and obey the Lord as they did and refuse to look back to your former life. That life is dead. There is no life found in the past, but in the present. We must not become irreverent of God's blessings and think that we too will escape the judgment our ancestors faced. How is it that there are generations of families that continue to be plagued by incarceration, unwanted pregnancies, and addiction? The latter generation said to themselves, "Oh, that will never happen to me" and thought they would get different results from the same behavior. As we discussed earlier, our enemy is the master of deception and will try to cause you to believe that you will still be blessed as you detour and go back to a land of bondage. We must realize that we have the power to do all things in Christ and realize that what we have in Christ is so much better than anything the world could offer. Though the world may provide temporary satisfaction, the joy and peace we have in Christ is eternal and lasting.

Anything of value in our life is going to require dedication and perseverance. Even the world recognizes that when you invest, you may not get a return immediately but in the end you expect to receive a greater portion than your original investment. Marriage, education, financial investments: all require commitment. I am so grateful that my mother invested in me and left me with the greatest inheritance I will ever have, which is my spiritual inheritance in Christ Jesus. Though there were periods of time where I may not have revealed the value of that investment, it paid off in the end. The Bible states to train up a child in the way that they should go and when they are older they will not turn away (Pr. 22:6). So expect some detours along the way, but in the end we should be on the right path. We all make mistakes but it's how we handle them that matters most. Repentance is more than accepting responsibility for our sin: it's accepting responsibility as well as not returning to that sin.

No one who puts is hand to the plow and looks back is
fit for service in the kingdom of God. (Lk. 9:62)

As Jesus was walking, men came to Him and said, "I will follow you wherever you go" and Jesus approached a man and said, "Follow me"(Lk. 9:57,59). The men desired to go but they first wanted to say goodbye to family and take care of other family business. Have we also given God excuses as to why we can't follow Him completely, right now? Jesus responded to them by saying how once we decide to follow Him we cannot look back: He is our number one priority. Everything else, even family, is secondary to the will of God in our lives. Perhaps the young Israelites glanced back as they entered into the Promised Land, because their hearts turned back as well. The problem with looking back is that it creates doubt as to whether or not we are doing the right thing. If we are sure in our decision there is no reason to look back. If I told someone that I was giving them the car of their dreams, handed them the keys, and showed them where it was, they wouldn't look back to say goodbye to their old car: they would immediately be on their way to get their new car. How is it that we run so quickly to worldly things, yet when it comes to the things of God we always second-guess ourselves? God tells us that if we seek Him first and His righteousness, He will provide for all our needs. So why do we not run to Him with abandonment? We will not move forward in God's will if we are constantly looking back at was and not looking forward to what has come. When God called Lot and his family to leave Sodom and Gomorrah, they were told to run quickly and not look back. Somewhere along the journey, Lot's wife looked back and instantly became a pillar of salt. Jesus tells the disciples that in the last days it will be the same way and no one should go back for anything. Jesus declares, "Remember Lot's wife!" (Lk. 17:32)

> *Whoever tries to keep his life will lose it, and whoever loses his life will preserve it. (Lk. 17:33)*

1. Do you find yourself looking back to past relationships, jobs, opportunities?

2. How can you enjoy each day to the fullest?

Prayer

Lord you are so awesome in all your ways. Every creation must give reverence to you. The mountains declare your glory and the oceans give you praise. I thank you for providing for my every need before I was even born. You gave me a divine purpose before I was even in my mother's womb. I will stand firm and walk in all that you have preordained for my life. Lord, I pray you utterly destroy every negative habit that threatens the will of God in my life. I pray that I will not be corrupted by ungodly counsel and communication. Every day let me die to my flesh and not succumb to the temptation of the enemy. Let me keep my eyes on you and not look back. I will not long for situations and relationships that you have called me to leave, for I am a new creature in Christ Jesus and all the former things have passed away. Lord, I pray that I seek you with an undivided heart, even in the midst of trying circumstances. Consume anything in my life that has occupied a space in my life that you desire to fill. Lord, give me a pure heart to serve you completely. Lord, I thank you that the vision you have for my life, though it may linger, it will come to pass. Amen.

CHAPTER 11

Making the Most of the Journey

Jesus bled and died not just to give us life, but to give it to us abundantly. It is God's will that we lack for nothing. Although we may have to overcome some mountains on our journey each day, we should make the most of everything God has given us. He has given us joy, peace, prosperity, favor, love, and so much more but it is up to us to access these blessings. God wants to bless us all. He has given us so many examples in His word of how He has used the least likely of people to do magnificent work for His kingdom. Joseph is a prime example of someone who made the most of his journey with God starting at a very young age.

JOSEPH'S JOURNEY TO LEADERSHIP

As a young boy Joseph always knew that he was called to do great things. He was the favored child of his father, Israel, formerly known as Jacob. Israel loved Joseph more than his other sons because he was born to him in his old age. To show his love for Joseph his father made him a brightly colored robe. According to tradition the eldest son, Reuben, should have received his father's blessing. However, God does not always follow the traditions of man. Jacob was also blessed above that of his brother Esau, even though he was the youngest. Time and time again God has shown that He is no respecter of persons and will favor who He chooses to favor, regardless of his or her position. The same was true when David was anointed king, although he was the youngest of his brothers. Just as David's brothers were jealous of their younger brothers, so to were Joseph's brothers jealous of him. The coat of many colors only made his brothers more jealous and hateful towards Joseph.

God began to reveal things to Joseph at an early age. In fact, Joseph was only about seventeen when God caused him to have the following dream. Joseph went to his brothers and said,

> There we were, binding sheaves in the field. Then behold, my sheaf arose and also stood upright, and indeed your sheaves stood all around and bowed down to my sheaf. (Gen.37:7)

Even if Joseph's brothers were not already jealous, his older brothers would not be excited to know that their little brother would rule over them. Now Joseph knew that his brothers were jealous of him, so what would he gain to tell him of his dream. He may have thought that they might respect him or perhaps even fall down and worship him right there, but neither happened. They just hated him all the more.

It appears that Joseph may have even enjoyed being favored over his brothers as he proceeded to tell him the next dream that he had. This time he told them that the sun, the moon, and eleven stars had bowed down before him. When he told his father, he rebuked him and said, "Do you expect your mother, your brothers, and I to bow down before you." His father's rebuke may reveal Joseph's arrogance in the statement of his dream. When God reveals that we are to lead for Him it is not so that we will be glorified, but that God be glorified in us.

Although his father rebuked Joseph, he still kept him in a favored position for he was allowed to stay at home, while his brothers went to graze their flocks. Israel told Joseph to go and check on his brothers and come back and let him know how they were doing. When his brothers saw him in the distance, in his special coat, they mocked him saying, "Here comes that dreamer!" They decided that they were tired of Joseph and his great dreams. His brothers plotted to kill him, but his oldest brother Reuben had mercy on Joseph and just put him in a pit, with the plan to go back and rescue him. They stripped Joseph of his special coat and did as Reuben said but then thought, "What will we gain from this?" So they took him and sold him to the Ishmaelites for twenty shekels of silver.

Why would Joseph's brothers be so jealous of him that they would want to kill him? Tension, jealousy, and strife had been present in their household their entire lives. The jealousy and envy had been passed down by their own mothers. Jacob had originally worked seven years to marry Rachel, but was tricked by her father and forced to marry Leah. Jacob loved Rachel more and God showed favor on Leah by opening her womb while Rachel's remained barren. Leah was the mother of Reuben, Simeon, Levi, Judah, Issachar, and Zebulun. Hurt, enraged, and envious Rachel gave her maidservant Bilhah to Jacob and she conceived Dan and Naphtali, which only created more tension. The Lord never forgot about Rachel and allowed her to conceive Joseph and Benjamin. However, after Leah's womb was barren she gave her maidservant, Zilpah to Jacob. Zilpah bore Gad and Asher. So there you have it four mothers, one husband, twelve sons, and a whole lot of drama. We have all experienced brother and sister rivalry even when they are both from the same parents or with parents in different households. Can you imagine all four mothers and children under one roof? From the time they were children one felt inferior because his mother was just a maidservant, or his mother was only second best. So when Joseph came along with his special coat and air of superiority they could not stand it. I believe they also feared that Joseph's dream would come true. Perhaps Joseph had other dreams that had come true before. Things that we doubt will happen do not usually bother us. They saw the favor that their father had given Joseph.

If you cannot be happy when one of your brothers or sisters in Christ is blessed or has God's favor, it reveals your own insecurity and lack of faith. What God has for you is for you, regardless of how He blesses others. The Bible tells us to rejoice with our brothers and sisters in Christ and to mourn when they mourn. We only hinder our own blessings when we are consumed with jealousy or wrath and it is impossible to please God without faith. We also must be patient that God will do what He has promised in His own time. If you are praying for a mate, don't be upset when someone else has found one before you. God knows what we can handle and when we can handle it. When God blessed Abraham with Isaac, He had to know that he would not love Isaac more than Himself. Abraham passed his test and revealed that he loved God more. Have we passed our test? When God has blessed us with something or someone, has our love for them surpassed our love for God? In loving that person or thing are you going against what you know God has called you to do? If so, God can allow us to be stripped of some things in order for us to be led by Him and not by our love for what He has given.

Though God revealed to Joseph that he would lead, he had to wait until his appointed time. First he had to learn how to follow. If Joseph began to think that his favor was because of who he was and not who God was in his life, it would hinder his ability to lead with humble spirit in obedience to God. David tells us "He guides the humble in what is right and teaches them his way"(Ps. 25:9).

God cannot lead us unless we are humble. If you were to look up the word humble in a dictionary you would find that it would represent someone who is not proud or haughty. One definition that I found particularly interesting is that one who is humble is unassuming. We cannot assume that we know everything and how God will do this or that, because His thoughts are so much higher than ours. Paul tells us that He is able to do so much more than we could ever ask or even think of, according to His power that works within us (Eph. 3:20). God may begin to reveal His will in our life but we cannot boast to others about it, because it has only been revealed in part. Like Joseph's brothers there will be those that will be jealous regardless, but we should not incite them with our pride. So we must come to God, as humble vessels that He can use to fulfill His will.

There are many gifts that God has given each and every one of us. Whether or not we realize it, God has given us talents but He has given it to us that we might glorify Him and not ourselves. The Bible reveals to us that some have been given the gift of wisdom, to some an extra measure of faith, to some the power to heal, and to some the gift of teaching or prophecy (I Cor. 12). Many of you have multiple gifts, some of which may not have been revealed. However, the same spirit has given all of our gifts and they should all work together to edify the body of Christ. This is why we should not be jealous of another's gift. No gift is more important than another; they all work together as do the parts of our human body. Nothing that happens to us will take away the gift that God has given to us. No hardship or unkind words can destroy what God has given us. Joseph's being sold into slavery would not deter God's plan for him to lead, but it would allow him to learn to be a follower so that he would lead with humility and not with pride.

Joseph was taken by the Ishmaelites and sold in Egypt to Potiphar, who was one of Pharaoh's officials. Joseph continued to have God's favor and Potiphar saw how he worked hard and God blessed him in all he did. So Joseph was given leadership over Potiphar's entire household. As Joseph grew to become a handsome young man, Potiphar's wife approached him and desired to sleep with him. Joseph overcame this test and literally ran away from her. Although he didwhat was right, Potiphar's wife lied and Joseph was sent to prison. Many times we think if we only do what is right all will be well. Yes, all will be well with our soul but we will still suffer for Christ's namesake, as he suffered for us. Christ did not suffer because of His sin, for He was perfect and upright in all His ways. We are blessed as we suffer for righteousness. Even in prison Joseph was given leadership and was blessed with the interpretation of dreams. As Joseph followed God he gave God all the glory for his success and did not seek glory for himself. When the men came to him for interpretations of their dreams, he stated, "Do not interpretations belong to God? Tell me your dreams" (Gen. 40:8). Joseph's confidence was not in his own ability but in God. There are gifts that we have not exercised in our own lives due to our lack of faith in God. Our Father wants to use us, but our faith is not strong enough for us to let Him. After Joseph interpreted their dreams, he only asked that the cupbearer remember him when he was restored to his position before Pharoah. After two years had passed, his former prison mate finally remembered Joseph request.

Pharaoh sent for Joseph to interpret his dreams and Joseph humbly replied, "I cannot do it, but God will give Pharaoh the answers he desires" (Gen. 41:16). Joseph explained to Pharaoh that there would be seven years of plenty and seven years of famine, so he must establish storehouses to collect food during the time of abundance. After his interpretation, Pharaoh saw that God favored Joseph and was convinced that there was no one in the land wiser than Joseph. Pharaoh took his signet ring from his finger and placed it on Joseph's finger. He appointed Joseph to be in charge of his entire palace, second in command only to Pharaoh himself. The people were required to respect Joseph as they would

Pharaoh. Pharaoh told Joseph, "I am Pharaoh, but without your word no one will lift hand or foot in all Egypt" (Gen. 41:44). He also gave Joseph Potiphera's daughter Asenath to be his wife. Joseph had two sons Manasseh, which means, "forget" in Hebrew, and Ephraim, which means "twice fruitful". Joseph was able to forget the pain of his past for he had more than he would ever need.

Joseph was thirty years old when he was appointed over Pharaoh's household. He was only seventeen when he was sold in to slavery and he spent many years in Pharaoh's prison for an act he didn't commit. There were probably times when Joseph was overwhelmed with sorrow while he was in prison. He did not ever know if he would marry or have a family of his own, or see his father again, but he did not lose faith in God. He probably remembered the dreams he had in his youth and may have continued to have dreams and wonder how God would fulfill them. If Joseph had taken his life in depression he would not been able to save thousands of lives.

God has a purpose for our lives and it would never be better if we were not here. We must never forget that God is faithful to complete what He has begun in us and when we may be at our lowest point, in an instance God will fulfill His promise to us and bless us so far above what we could even think of. God knows everything in advanced and will use our hardships as a footstool to our blessing. Nothing can deter God's plan for our lives. No weapon formed against us will prosper, for with God all things work together for the good of those that love Him and are called according to His purpose.

Joseph fulfilled his divine calling because he did not compromise his convictions or take advantage of the favor God had given him. After his master's wife repeatedly tried to tempt him day after day, he could have said maybe one kiss would be enough for her to leave me alone. However, that one kiss may have led to much more, perhaps even pregnancy as it did for David. He would have altered God's will in his life by his own sinful nature. Joseph stood strong against temptation and humbled himself before God, he could complete God's divine will for his life. Many people have never fulfilled their divine calling because they have continued to compromise in the directions that God has given them. If God tells you not to do something it is only because He sees the final outcome and what He has planned for you. Others may say it's okay, it's no big deal, but their calling is not you're calling. So stand firm on what God has told you to do and do not let the enemy steer you away from what God has already purposed for you to accomplish.

> *Your beginnings will seem humble, so prosperous will your future be (Job 8:7).*

DON'T BE DISCOURAGED BY HUMBLE BEGINNINGS

Many people fail to make the most of their journey when they think that they are not worthy to be used by God. David was just a little shepherd boy but because of his great faith he was exalted to be a King. While Joseph was in jail he could have given up on God and his great visions, but he continued to give God glory and honor. He could have become embittered and hateful after he was wrongfully accused but he still desired to bless others and was given leadership and favor even in jail. We have to learn as Paul did that regardless of the circumstance we will learn to be content in all situations, knowing that we can do all things through Christ that strengthens us. Many read Philippians 4:13, "we can do all things through Christ" and fail to put in context that by "all things" that includes both good and bad. Paul explains earlier in times of lack and in times of plenty. Paul was actually in prison when he wrote Philippians. We often tend to use that verse only to mean give us strength to do what we desire to do. But even when we are in jobs that we don't desire we must learn what it means to be content and know that God can use us in any situation.

> *Humble yourselves, therefore, under God's mighty hand, that he may lift you up in due time. (I Pet. 5:6)*

1. Are there areas that you may need to be more humble?

2. How can you be more faithful to God even in small things?

Prayer

Heavenly Father, I thank you for the dreams you have given to me. I know you are faithful to complete every good work that you have begun in me. Lord, let me not be discouraged by the negative reports of others. Forgive those who have sought to steal the vision you have placed in my heart. Let me not hold bitterness toward anyone. I know that all things will work for my good as I seek your perfect will for my life. Lord, guide be by your wisdom and let me hear clearly what steps to take in fulfilling all that you have set out for me to do. I thank you for the times of struggle that have humbled me, strengthened me, and prepared me for a holy calling. Forgive me for areas that I have not been faithful. Father, my desire is to please you in all that I do. Give me the strength to walk by faith and not by sight.

CHAPTER 12

The Finish Line

Trophies aren't given for great starts. Medals aren't awarded for entering the race. A good start is crucial, but in the end, the end is all that matters.

– Max Lucado

How will we end our journey? Will we run the race God has given us with no goal or objective in mind? Will we look back with regret and disappointment? I pray not. Not when we have been given instructions in God's word on how to live a victorious life. Regardless of how humble our beginnings are, our end should be greater than our beginning. We hear of musicians, athletes, businessmen, and actors who have attained the highest levels of success, yet died penniless and alone. This is not how the end of the righteous will be. Your life of faith should leave an inheritance for generations to come, as it did for Abraham. Solomon, one of the wisest and wealthiest men of his time stated, "The end of a the thing is better than the beginning; the patient in spirit is better than the proud in spirit" (Eccl. 7: 8). We should be bet-

ter at the end than we were at the beginning. We should be
wiser, stronger, and closer to God than ever before.

RUTH'S JOURNEY FROM ASHES TO BEAUTY

One woman in the Bible who ended in such a manner
was Ruth. In the lineage of Christ, you will find the story of
Ruth. Ruth was one of the least likely candidates you would
expect to be used in such an extraordinary way. First of all,
Ruth was not even a Hebrew, nor were any members of her
family. She was introduced to the God of Israel when she
married Mahlon, son of Elimelech and Naomi. As she devel-
oped a close-knit bond with Naomi she began to share her
love and her faith. We must first understand how unusual it
was for Naomi to love her foreign daughter-in-laws as her
own daughters. Today, people with different backgrounds
and religions get married without giving it a second thought,
but according to Israelite faith marrying foreign women was
an abominable act. Mosaic Law even forbade an Ammonite
or Moabite to enter into the congregation of the Lord (Deut.
23:3). Another example given in the Bible that shows the
seriousness of this issue is in Abraham's fervent request to
his faithful servant. Abraham called his servant to him and
made him swear by the Lord, God of heaven and earth, that
he would not allow his beloved son, Isaac, to marry one of
the Canaanite women, but that he would go to his home-
land among his people and find a wife for Isaac (Gen. 24:
4). Despite the history of prejudice and disdain for foreign-
ers, Naomi did not reject Ruth. Ruth would in turn show
her gratefulness in pledging her life to Ruth and serving her
God.

Naomi was not the only one who had to reject the opinions of others and walk away from family and friends. Ruth also had to abandon her family, her faith, and her customs. We don't know the rejection Ruth may have felt by marrying an Israelite man. All parents have hopes and dreams for their children. There was probably a wealthy Moabite young man who was a friend of the family and a perfect match for Ruth, in their eyes. First of all Mahlon was puny, that is literally what the translation of his name means. He may have always been sickly and tiny since his birth. So he wasn't much to look at and his family would not meet the approval of their friends. They ate differently, they talked differently, and they were not able to relate to them like they would with another Moabite family. So Ruth faced rejection on both sides from her own family as well as from the Israelite community. She gave up everything to be with Mahlon and then he died. Can you imagine the pain and loneliness she must have felt? After the death of Mahlon she was rejected by her own family and then her mother-in-law told her to go. Naomi had lost her husband and both sons. She did not want to burden her daughter-in-laws with the possibility of being widows forever. She would not be able to have other sons for them to marry and even if she did would they wait for them to be old enough to marry? Orpah, the widow of Chilion, agreed to go back but Ruth proclaimed,

> *Don't urge me to leave you or to turn back from you.*
> *Where you go I will go, and where you stay I will stay.*
> *Your people will be my people and your God my God.*
> *Where you die I will die, and there I will be buried. May*

the Lord deal with me, be it ever so severely, if anything
but death separates you and me. (Ruth 1: 16-17,NIV)

SHE DIED IN ORDER TO LIVE.

We fail to acknowledge the sacrifice Ruth made to return with Naomi to Bethlehem. Although she faced ridicule from her family and friends in Moab, she faced the worst kind of scrutiny as a Moabitess in the holy land of Bethlehem. She was rejected, scorned, abused, misunderstood, and yet she placed Naomi's needs above her own. Surely she could have returned home. Her family would have accepted and comforted her in her time of loss. They would have been excited to have her back and perhaps able to see their initial plans for her prevail. Yet, Ruth was able to see that what she had gained in knowing Naomi and knowing her God was worth losing it all. She was more than willing to leave her place of comfort in order to stay in God's presence.

Our journey with God will always push us further and further away from our comfort zones, in order that we might know God more fully. We may believe in our mind that God is able to do all things. But when we have no one else to turn to and we have come to the end of ourselves it is God alone who makes a way out of no way. It is then that we know in our hearts that He is more than able to complete the work he has begun in us. Ruth had to move into an unfamiliar land in order to see God's favor and love for her. Many times we desire to know God more fully and see Him more clearly, but we don't want to chase after Him. We don't want to grope for Him in the dark and make our way in unfamiliar territory.

We want to stay right where we are in the same mindset, with the same people, doing the same thing, and yet expect God to move mightily. We must realize that wherever He leads us will bring us closer to Him and cause us to know Him more fully. Yes, He will test us and reveal our own insecurities and fears, but through the testing we will grow and become more like Him.

When we die to our agenda, our flesh, our self-ambition, somehow God resurrects us to walk in His Glory. So that all we lost we consider it nothing in comparison to what we have gained in knowing Him and who we are able to be in His might. We will never know our full capability until God stretches us beyond our present limitations. As we surrender to His will and die to our own, He is magnified in us and through us.

SHE REMAINED FAITHFUL IN THE MIDST OF OPPOSITION.

But without faith it is impossible to please Him, for he who comes to God must believe that He is, and that He is a rewarder of those who diligently seek Him . (Heb. 11:6)

As Ruth served Naomi, she was able to show her the unconditional love that God has for us. Even when Naomi was bitter and ungrateful, Ruth remained hopeful and diligent. Regardless of her condition or the condition of the people around her, she remained faithful to the work God gave her to do. Ruth was not swayed by the fact that Orpah went back. She was determined to do what God had called her to do regardless of what others may have said or done. Ruth didn't let others stop her from fulfilling her mission, not even Naomi. When Naomi saw that Ruth was wholeheartedly determined to follow her she stopped trying to convince her.

In order for us to complete our mission we to must be diligent and determined to fulfill the vision God has given us. Our friends may decide to walk in another direction, but we must remain faithful even when our journey looks hopeless and impossible. When we are steadfast in pursuing the purpose God has for our lives without wavering or doubting, those who had once tried to persuade us to go back will be convinced that we are not going to let anyone or anything stop us from fulfilling the work God has given us to do.

Ruth went with Naomi on a journey that looked pretty hopeless. However, I believe that Ruth could see beyond the seemingly hopeless situation and see all the possibilities in God. In fact, Ruth declared and walked her blessings before she even received them. When Ruth and Naomi arrived in Bethlehem, Ruth stated that she would go to a field in which "I will find grace." It is so important to declare the favor of the Lord over our lives. There was no reason for Ruth to believe that she would find grace or favor with anyone. She was a foreigner considered less than one of their servants. When she stepped out on faith, God ordered her steps so that she just didn't go to any field, but to the field of Boaz who was a near relative of Naomi's husband, Elimelech. Ruth worked so faithfully gleaning bundles of grain that Boaz had to ask who she was. Boaz showed her kindness from the moment he met her. Ruth then asked Boaz for favor in his sight and immediately she received it as Boaz invited her to eat with him and his workers. He commanded his workers to allow extra grain to fall for her to gather.

Ruth pressed on and passed every test of her faith with complete obedience. When Naomi realized the favor Boaz bestowed on Ruth, she knew it was by no coincidence that she was gleaning in his field, but that there was a greater blessing God had in store. Naomi knew that Boaz would be the one to provide for Ruth and redeem their family name. She told Ruth what she would need to do to request that Boaz serve as their family redeemer. What Naomi told Ruth to do would test her faith as she faced the possibility of rejection and dishonor. Ruth went to where Boaz was working and waited in the dark until after he had fallen asleep and then uncovered his feet and laid down. Of course Boaz was startled when he awoke to her presence but even more surprised by her request. Boaz stated,

> *For you have shown more kindness at the end than at the beginning, in that you did not go after young men, whether poor or rich. And now, my daughter, do not fear. I will do for you all that you request, for all the people of my town know you are a virtuous woman. (Ruth 3:10-11)*

God used Naomi to push Ruth into her blessing. We could be right in the place of our blessing and don't even realize it until someone else reveals it to us. Although Boaz may not have been the perfect man that Ruth pictured in her mind, he was all that she wanted and more. Many of us miss our blessing by waiting for them to come in perfect little packages and God wants us to see if our faith is strong enough to see beyond the packaging. Ruth finally received the highest favor in Boaz's eyes as he claimed her as his wife. Even after she risked her reputation and the possibility of complete rejection by Boaz she still had to wait for one matter to be settled. Before Boaz could marry Ruth and redeem her family name he had to consult with another closer family member to see if he desired to redeem her. This shows the man of integrity that Boaz was. Though he was overjoyed with the possibility of having a wife that he had prayed so many years for, he first did what was right in the eyes of the law. Ruth faced the possibility of having to marry a complete stranger. Even after she had done what God had called her to do, she had one last test before she could receive the abundant blessing God had ordained for her. When Boaz presented the matter before the relative he was eager to claim the land, but rejected the offer when he found out that he would have to take Ruth as well. Maybe he rejected her because she was a Moabitess. Maybe he did not want to give Elimelech's inheritance to their future son, which he would be required to do as the redeemer. Maybe he simply wasn't attracted to her. Whatever the reason, it was necessary for him to reject Ruth in order for God to bless her tremendously.

We often become so discouraged and feel that God has forgotten us when we are rejected by others. When, in fact, it is because God has remembered us and what He has ordained for our lives. He allows others to reject us so He can bless us. When we don't get the job we wanted, it is only because God has something better in store. When relationships fail, we must know that God has something better in store.

When Mahlon died Ruth did not stop living, she moved on. When she moved on and followed God she was blessed with more than she ever thought was possible. We have to understand that God has already worked out everything for our good when we are walking according to His purpose for our lives. Ruth remained faithful even in the midst of rejection and denial. In the end she left a legacy that exceeded beyond her lifetime. From generation to generation her story will inspire others to walk by faith and not by sight. We, too, must not be afraid to step out in faith and leave our areas of comfort in order to walk in all that God has ordained for us. Christ said that He came to give us life more abundantly. In order to walk in His abundance we must be willing to give it all away. Then God knows He has our heart and He can trust us with His blessing. Although you may risk being rejected, ridiculed, hurt, frustrated, embarrassed, and even persecuted in the end you will reap the blessings of joy, abundance, favor, and honor before God and man. Just as a woman gives birth, the pain of labor is incomparable to the joy of being a mother. Continue to push until you reach the place of blessing God has predestined just for you.

1. Is there anyone in your life who is not helping you to fulfill your mission?

2. Who has God placed in your life to help you reach your destiny?

Prayer

*Lord, you said where much is given, much is required.
You have given me knowledge of who I am in Christ
and know it is my responsibility to walk accordingly.
Lord help me to attain my highest potential in you. I
realize this requires me to be stretched beyond what I
can accomplish in my own strength. I thank you for
those you have sent and will send to strengthen me. Let
the power of your Holy Spirit also strengthen me as I
diligently seek your will for my life. I know you will
bless me in order that I might be a blessing. At the end
of my life, let people remember me for the love I have
shown to others, for the integrity of my character, and
for the passion I had in serving you. Let me not look
back with regret and shame. I thank you for the people
you have put in my life to encourage me and push me to
walk in all that you have for me. Let me see life through
your eyes and realize the awesome blessings you have
placed before me. Let me not dwell on past hurts, but
appreciate the life you have given me today. I thank you
for answering my prayer. AMEN.*

Suggested Reading

Listen to Your Life, Valorie Burton

Deliver Me From Adam, Bishop Eddie Long

Prayer, O. Hallesby

Maximize the Moment, Bishop T.D. Jakes

The Pursuit of Holiness, Jerry Bridges

Life on the Edge, James Dobson

My Utmost for His Highest, Oswald Chambers

About the Author

Tonia East has been working with young adults and college-age adults professionally for eight years. She is currently working with new adults as the Speech Program Coordinator and professor of Speech Communication, in which she teaches Public Speaking, Voice and Diction, and Business and Professional Communication. She also works with junior high and high school youth. Ms. East is an accomplished public speaker and is invited to speak to young adults and new adults about spiritual issues as well as ways to communicate more effectively in relationships, business, or family situations.

All of these experiences have increased her awareness of the issues this generation faces and of the questions that need to be answered. As she has shared her experiences with her students, they have revealed their own insecurities, failures, and aspirations. Each semester there is a student that has attempted suicide and each semester there is a student that is dealing with substance abuse. Changing Lanes was written to give these students hope and direction as they navigate their way through life.

To contact Ms. East for questions, comments, and for speaking engagements she may be reached at the following addresses:

Tonia East
P.O. Box 92157
Atlanta, GA 30314
teast@palacommunication.com

CPSIA information can be obtained at www.ICGtesting.com
Printed in the USA
LVOW08s0115140816

500307LV00001B/10/P